W9-CRI-094

Java EE 6
Pocket Guide

Arun Gupta

O'REILLY®

Beijing · Cambridge · Farnham · Köln · Sebastopol · Tokyo

Java EE 6 Pocket Guide
by Arun Gupta

Copyright © 2012 Arun Gupta. All rights reserved.
Printed in the United States of America.

Published by O'Reilly Media, Inc., 1005 Gravenstein Highway North, Sebastopol, CA 95472.

O'Reilly books may be purchased for educational, business, or sales promotional use. Online editions are also available for most titles (*http://my.safari booksonline.com*). For more information, contact our corporate/institutional sales department: 800-998-9938 or *corporate@oreilly.com*.

Editors: Mike Loukides and Meghan Blanchette
Copyeditor: Emily Quill
Production Editor: Kristen Borg
Proofreader: Kiel Van Horn
Indexer: Lucie Haskins
Cover Designer: Karen Montgomery
Interior Designer: David Futato
Illustrator: Rebecca Demarest

September 2012:   First Edition.

Revision History for the First Edition:
    2012-09-10   First release
See *http://oreilly.com/catalog/errata.csp?isbn=9781449336684* for release details

Nutshell Handbook, the Nutshell Handbook logo, and the O'Reilly logo are registered trademarks of O'Reilly Media, Inc. *Java EE 6 Pocket Guide*, the image of a jellyfish (*Favonia octonema*), and related trade dress are trademarks of O'Reilly Media, Inc.

Many of the designations used by manufacturers and sellers to distinguish their products are claimed as trademarks. Where those designations appear in this book, and O'Reilly Media, Inc., was aware of a trademark claim, the designations have been printed in caps or initial caps.

While every precaution has been taken in the preparation of this book, the publisher and author assume no responsibility for errors or omissions, or for damages resulting from the use of the information contained herein.

ISBN: 978-1-449-33668-4

[M]

1347291167

To Menka,
my lovely wife and
best friend. Your
support and encour-
agement make our
lives fun and
meaningful.

To
Aditya and Mihir,
my two joyful boys,
for playing with me
and keeping me
charged.

Contents

Preface

The Java EE 6 platform has taken ease-of-development in enterprise Java programming to new heights. This book is directed towards the audience who wants to get a quick overview of the platform and to keep coming back to learn the basics.

This book provides an overview of the key specifications in the Java EE 6 platform (one specification per chapter). The main concepts from the different specifications are explained and accompanied by code samples. No prior knowledge of earlier versions of the platform is required. However, some basic understanding of Java is required to understand the code.

Conventions Used in This Book

The following typographical conventions are used in this book:

Italic

> Indicates new terms, URLs, email addresses, filenames, and file extensions.

`Constant width`

> Used for program listings, as well as within paragraphs to refer to program elements such as variable or function names, databases, data types, environment variables, statements, and keywords.

Constant width italic

Shows text that should be replaced with user-supplied values or by values determined by context.

Using Code Examples

This book is here to help you get your job done. In general, you may use the code in this book in your programs and documentation. You do not need to contact us for permission unless you're reproducing a significant portion of the code. For example, writing a program that uses several chunks of code from this book does not require permission. Selling or distributing a CD-ROM of examples from O'Reilly books does require permission. Answering a question by citing this book and quoting example code does not require permission. Incorporating a significant amount of example code from this book into your product's documentation does require permission.

We appreciate, but do not require, attribution. An attribution usually includes the title, author, publisher, and ISBN. For example: "*Java EE 6 Pocket Guide* by Arun Gupta (O'Reilly). Copyright 2012 Arun Gupta, 978-1-449-33668-4."

If you feel your use of code examples falls outside fair use or the permission given above, feel free to contact us at *permissions@oreilly.com*.

Safari® Books Online

 Safari Books Online (*www.safaribookson line.com*) is an on-demand digital library that delivers expert content in both book and video form from the world's leading authors in technology and business.

Technology professionals, software developers, web designers, and business and creative professionals use Safari Books

Online as their primary resource for research, problem solving, learning, and certification training.

Safari Books Online offers a range of product mixes and pricing programs for organizations, government agencies, and individuals. Subscribers have access to thousands of books, training videos, and prepublication manuscripts in one fully searchable database from publishers like O'Reilly Media, Prentice Hall Professional, Addison-Wesley Professional, Microsoft Press, Sams, Que, Peachpit Press, Focal Press, Cisco Press, John Wiley & Sons, Syngress, Morgan Kaufmann, IBM Redbooks, Packt, Adobe Press, FT Press, Apress, Manning, New Riders, McGraw-Hill, Jones & Bartlett, Course Technology, and dozens more. For more information about Safari Books Online, please visit us online.

How to Contact Us

Please address comments and questions concerning this book to the publisher:

> O'Reilly Media, Inc.
> 1005 Gravenstein Highway North
> Sebastopol, CA 95472
> 800-998-9938 (in the United States or Canada)
> 707-829-0515 (international or local)
> 707-829-0104 (fax)

We have a web page for this book, where we list errata, examples, and any additional information. You can access this page at *http://oreil.ly/javaEE6-pocketguide*.

To comment or ask technical questions about this book, send email to *bookquestions@oreilly.com*.

For more information about our books, courses, conferences, and news, see our website at *http://www.oreilly.com*.

Find us on Facebook: *http://facebook.com/oreilly*

Follow us on Twitter: *http://twitter.com/oreillymedia*

Watch us on YouTube: *http://www.youtube.com/oreillymedia*

Acknowledgments

This book was not possible without support from a multitude of people.

First and foremost, many thanks to O'Reilly for trusting in me and providing an opportunity to write this book. Their team provided excellent support throughout the editing, reviewing, proofreading, and publishing process.

At O'Reilly, Michael Loukides helped me with bootstrapping the book. Meghan Blanchette provided excellent editorial help throughout all the stages, helping with interim reviews, providing feedback on styling, arranging technical reviews, and connecting me with the rest of the team when required. Jessica Hosman helped me in getting started and guided the authoring process.

Emily Quill and Kristen Borg helped with copyediting and making sure to provide the finishing touches. And thanks to the rest of the O'Reilly team with whom I did not interact directly, but were helping in many other ways.

The detailed proofreading and technical review by Markus Eisele (@myfear, *http://blog.eisele.net*), John Yeary (@jyeary, *http://javaevangelist.blogspot.com*), and Bert Ertman (@Bert Ertman, *http://bertertman.wordpress.com*) ensured that the relevant content was covered accurately. Their vast experience and knowledge showed in the depth of their comments.

I am grateful for the numerous discussions with developers around the world that helped me understand the technology better. Thanks to my colleagues at Oracle and the JSR specification leads for explaining the intended use cases of different technologies. And thanks to everybody else in my life, who provided much-needed breaks from book writing.

CHAPTER 1

Java Platform, Enterprise Edition

Introduction

The Java Platform, Enterprise Edition (Java EE) provides a standards-based platform for developing web and enterprise applications. These applications are typically designed as multitier applications, with a frontend tier consisting of web frameworks, a middle tier providing security and transactions, and a backend tier providing connectivity to a database or a legacy system. The Java EE platform defines APIs for different components in each tier, and also provides some additional services such as naming, injection, and resource management that span across the platform. Each component is defined in a separate specification that also describes the API, javadocs, and expected behavior.

The Java Platform, Enterprise Edition 6 (Java EE 6) was released in December 2009 and provides a simple, easy-to-use, and complete stack for building such applications. The previous version of the platform, Java EE 5, took the first step in providing a simplified developer experience. The Java EE 6 platform further improves upon the developer productivity features and also adds a lot more functionality.

The three main goals of the platform are:

Ease of use

> The Java EE 6 platform takes ease of use to new heights by extensively using convention over configuration and heavy use of annotations on a Plain Old Java Object (POJO). Adding `@Stateless`, `@Stateful`, or `@Singleton` to a POJO makes it an Enterprise JavaBean. Further, this could be easily packaged in a WAR file instead of a special packaging of JAR or EAR. Servlets are POJOs as well, annotated with `@WebServlet`. Deployment descriptors like `web.xml` and `faces-config.xml` are optional in most cases; the information typically specified in deployment descriptors is now captured in annotations. There are default rules of navigation from one page of JSF to another. Publishing a POJO as a RESTful web service is equivalent to adding an `@Path` annotation on a POJO.
>
> Making deployment descriptors optional, using convention over configuration, and relying heavily on annotations makes the Java EE 6 platform easy to use and, above all, less verbose.

Lightweight

> There are 31 component specifications in the Java EE 6 platform, as listed in Appendix EE.6 of the platform specification. These components include Enterprise JavaBeans (EJB), Servlets, JavaServer Faces (JSF), Java API for RESTful Web Services (JAX-RS), and many others. Building a typical enterprise application may not require all the components. Also, some of the technologies like Java API for XML Registries (JAXR) or Java API for XML-based RPC (JAX-RPC) were very relevant when introduced in the platform. Now they have either been replaced by better components, such as Java API for XML Web Services (JAX-WS), or are no longer used.
>
> The Java SE Expert Group defined a two-step process for removing features from the platform. In this process, known as *pruning*, a feature is marked as optional (referred to as *proposed optional*) in one release, and then a

subsequent release can decide to either remove the feature, retain it as a required component, or leave it in the *proposed removal* state. The Java EE Expert Group used that process and targeted some features for pruning. This is analogous to trimming rose bushes in the beginning of each year so that fresh blossoms can grow. Pruning unused features ensures that even with new feature additions, the platform will remain simple and lightweight.

The Java EE platform also introduces the notion of *profiles*. A profile represents a configuration of the platform suited to a particular class of applications. A profile may be a subset or superset of the technologies in the platform. The Java EE 6 Web Profile is defined as a separate specification in the platform, and is defined as a subset of technologies contained in the platform and targeted toward the developers of modern web applications. This breaks away from the "one size fits all" approach of previous releases. And although it's a proper subset, it still offers a reasonably complete stack composed of standard APIs, and it's capable out-of-the-box for addressing a wide variety of web applications. The web profile allows developers to build web applications quickly and prevents the proliferation of custom web stacks for easier maintainability. Additional profiles can be defined by following the rules of the Java Community Process (JCP).

Together, pruning and web profiles make the Java EE 6 platform lightweight and simple to maintain.

Extensibility

The platform provides a rich set of functionality to create enterpise applications. However, it's a common practice to include third-party frameworks to supplement or complement functionality in the platform. These frameworks require registration of a `ServletListener`, `ServletFilter`, or similar component so that they are recognized by the runtime. The Servlet specification defines a *web fragment* mechanism by which these entry points to the framework are defined in the framework library. The Servlet containers then register the framework, relieving the developer of the burden. This allows these frameworks to be treated as first-class citizens of the platform.

In addition, the Contexts and Dependency Injection (CDI) specification defines a portable extension mechanism that allows you to extend the capabilities of the platform in different ways, for example by providing certain predefined scopes. A new scope can be easily defined and included with any Java EE 6–compliant application server using the portable extensions method.

Specifications like CDI, JavaServer Faces 2, Java API for RESTful Services, Java Persistence API 2, and Servlets 3 make the Java EE 6 platform more powerful. This book will provide an overview of the main technologies included in the platform, and easy-to-understand code samples will be used throughout to demonstrate improvements in Java EE 6.

Deliverables

The Java EE 6 platform was developed as Java Specification Request 316 or JSR 316 (*http://jcp.org/en/jsr/detail?id=316*) following Java Community Process (JCP) 2.7. The JCP process defines three key deliverables for any JSR:

Specification
> A formal document that describes the proposed component and its features.

Reference Implementation (RI)
> Binary implementation of the proposed specification. The RI helps to ensure that the proposed specifications can be implemented in a binary form and provides constant feedback to the specification process.

Technology Compliance Kit (TCK)
> A set of tests that verify that the RI is in compliance with the specification. This allows multiple vendors to provide compliant implementations.

Java EE 6 consists of the platform specification that defines requirements across the platform. It also consists of the following component specifications:

Web Technologies

- JSR 45: Debugging Support for Other Languages
- JSR 52: Standard Tag Library for JavaServer Pages (JSTL)1.2
- JSR 245: JavaServer Pages (JSP) 2.2 and Expression Language (EL) 1.2
- JSR 314: JavaServer Faces (JSF) 2.0
- JSR 315: Servlet 3.0

Enterprise Technologies

- JSR 250: Common Annotations for the Java Platform 1.1
- JSR 299: Contexts and Dependency Injection (CDI) for the Java EE Platform 1.0
- JSR 303: Bean Validation 1.0
- JSR 316: Managed Beans 1.0
- JSR 317: Java Persistence API (JPA) 2.0
- JSR 318: Enterprise JavaBeans (EJB) 3.1
- JSR 318: Interceptors 1.1
- JSR 322: Java EE Connector Architecture 1.6
- JSR 330: Dependency Injection for Java 1.0
- JSR 907: Java Transaction API (JTA) 1.1
- JSR 914: Java Message Server (JMS) 1.1
- JSR 919: JavaMail 1.4

Web Service Technologies

- JSR 67: Java APIs for XML Messaging (JAXM) 1.3
- JSR 93: Java API for XML Registries (JAXR) 1.0
- JSR 101: Java API for XML-based RPC (JAX-RPC) 1.1
- JSR 109: Implementing Enterprise Web Services 1.3

- JSR 173: Streaming API for XML (StAX) 1.0
- JSR 181: Web Services Metadata for the Java Platform 2.0
- JSR 222: Java Architecture for XML Binding (JAXB) 2.2
- JSR 224: Java API for XML Web Services (JAX-WS) 2.2
- JSR 311: Java API for RESTful Web Services (JAX-RS) 1.1

Management and Security Technologies

- JSR 77: J2EE Management API 1.1
- JSR 88: Java Platform EE Application Deployment API 1.2
- JSR 115: Java Authorization Contract and Containers (JACC) 1.3
- JSR 196: Java Authentication Service Provider Inteface for Containers (JASPIC) 1.0

The different components work together to provide an integrated stack, as shown in Figure 1-1.

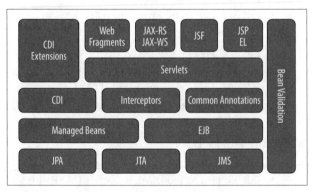

Figure 1-1. Java EE 6 architecture

In Figure 1-1:

- JPA, JTA, and JMS provide the basic services such as database access, transactions, and messaging.

- Managed Beans and EJB provide a simplified programming model using POJOs to use the basic services.

- CDI, Interceptors, and Common Annotations provide concepts that are applicable to a wide variety of components, such as type-safe dependency injection, addressing cross-cutting concerns using interceptors, and a common set of annotations.

- CDI Extensions allow you to extend the platform beyond its existing capabilities in a standard way.

- Web services using JAX-RS and JAX-WS, JSF, JSP, and EL define the programming model for web applications. Web Fragments allow automatic registration of third-party web frameworks in a very natural way.

- Bean Validation provides a standard means to declare constraints and validate them across different technologies.

JAX-RPC (JSR 101), JAXR (JSR 93), EJB Entity Beans (part of JSR 153), and Java EE Application Deployment (JSR 88) are marked for pruning in this version of the platform.

The RI of Java EE 6 is built in the GlassFish Community. The GlassFish Server Open Source Edition provides a full Java EE 6–compliant, free, and open source application server. It is also available in a Web Profile distribution and can be downloaded from *http://glassfish.org*. The application server is easy to use (zip installer and NetBeans/Eclipse/IntelliJ integration), lightweight (downloads starting at 30 MB, small disk/memory footprint), and modular (OSGi-based, containers start on demand). It also provides clustering with high availability and centralized administration using CLI, web-based administration console, and REST management/monitoring APIs. The Oracle GlassFish Server is Oracle's commercially supported GlassFish server distribution and can be downloaded from *http://oracle.com/goto/glassfish*. As of this writing, there are 17 Java EE 6–compliant application servers. The complete list is available at *http://www.oracle.com/technetwork/java/javaee/overview/compatibility-jsp-136984.html*.

The TCK is available to all Java EE licensees for testing their respective implementations.

What's New in Java EE 6

Some new specifications have been added to improve the functionality and richness of the platform. Several existing component specifications were revised to make them simple and easy to use.

The main features of the key specifications are described.

Managed Beans

- POJO-based managed component.
- Provides common set of services such as lifecycle resource injection, callbacks, and interceptors.

Enterprise JavaBeans

- An EJB can be created with a single source file per bean and annotated with `@Stateless`, `@Stateful`, or `@Singleton`.
- EJBs can be packaged in a `.war` for local access using `@Local` and `ejb-jar` for local and remote access.
- EJBs can be accessed using a portable global JNDI name.
- A method of a session bean may be marked to be invoked asynchronously. These methods allow the client to retrieve the result value later, or use the fire-and-forget pattern.
- Time-based events can be scheduled using cron-like syntax by specifying `@Schedule` on bean methods.

- The Embeddable EJB API allows client code and its corresponding enterprise beans to run within the same JVM and the class loader.

Servlets

- Annotation-driven Servlet (`@WebServlet`), Filter (`@Web Filter`), and Listener (`@WebListener`). The `web.xml` descriptor becomes optional in most of the common cases.

- Servlets, filters, and listeners can be programmatically registered using `ServletContext`.

- Asynchronous servlets allow the control (or thread) to return back to the container to perform other tasks while waiting for the long-running process to complete.

- Framework libraries can be integrated in a modular way using `web-fragment.xml`.

- Servlet security can be specified using `@ServletSecu rity`, `@HttpConstraint`, and `@HttpMethodConstraint` in addition to `<security-constraint>`.

Java API for RESTful Web Services

- POJO-based and annotation-driven way of publishing RESTful web services.

- Standard set of HTTP protocol methods such as GET, POST, PUT, and DELETE are supported.

- Each resource can be represented in multiple formats; custom types are supported as well.

- Client-side content negotiation supported using HTTP `Accept:` header.

SOAP-Based Web Services

- Publish SOAP-based web services using a POJO and annotations. Finer grained control over the messages using `Source`, `DataSource`, and `SOAPMessage`.

- Client-side API to invoke a SOAP-based web service.

- Well-defined extension points for pre/post processing of request/response messages on client and server.
- Standard Java-to-WSDL and WSDL-to-Java mapping.

JavaServer Faces

- Facelets is defined as the preferred templating language for the page. This allows composite components to be easily defined, enabling true abstraction.
- Support for Ajax using JavaScript APIs and declarative Ajax using `f:ajax`.
- Most of the elements in `faces-config.xml` have an alternative annotation. Default navigation rules are defined following convention-over-configuration.
- HTTP GET support and bookmarkable URLs.
- Integration with Bean Validation.

Java Persistence API

- An improved object/relational mapping to provide more intuitive Java mapping. An expanded and richer JPQL to support the improved mapping and some new functionality.
- The Metamodel captures a metamodel of the persistent state and relationships of the managed classes of a persistence unit. This abstract persistence schema is then used to author the type-safe queries using Criteria API.
- Pessimistic locking is supported in addition to optimistic locking by the addition of new locking modes.
- Standard configuration options using `javax.persistence` properties.

Interceptors

- Interpose on invocations and lifecycle events that occur on an associated target class.
- Interceptors can be applied using annotations such as `@Interceptors` or in a type-safe manner using a deployment descriptor such as `beans.xml`.

Contexts and Dependency Injection

- Standards-based type-safe dependency injection.
- Provides strong typing by specifying all dependencies using Java type system. Provides loose coupling with Events, Interceptors, and Decorators.
- Provides an integration with Expression Language.
- Defines an extensible scope and context management mechanism.
- Bridges transactional tier (EJB) and presentation tier (JSF) in the platform.

Bean Validation

- Class-level constraint declaration and validation facility for POJOs.
- Provides a built-in set of constraint definitions such as `@NotNull`, `@Min`, `@Max`, and `@Size`.
- Custom constraints can be declared using *META-INF/validation.xml* in addition to annotations.

CHAPTER 2

Managed Beans

Managed Beans is defined as part of JSR 316, and the complete specification can be downloaded from *http://jcp.org/aboutJava/communityprocess/final/jsr316/index.html*.

A managed bean is a POJO that is treated as a managed component by a Java EE container. It provides a common foundation for different kinds of components that exist in the Java EE platform. In addition, the specification also defines a small set of basic services such as resource injection, lifecycle callbacks, and interceptors on these beans.

Different component specifications can add other characteristics to this managed bean. The specification even defines well-known extension points to modify some aspects. For example, Contexts and Dependency Injection (CDI) relaxes the requirement to have a POJO with a no-args constructor, and allows constructors with more complex signatures. CDI also adds support for lifecycle scopes and events. Similarly, Enterprise JavaBeans is a managed bean and adds support for transactions and other services. This allows the developer to start light and create a more powerful component such as an EJB or CDI bean if and when the need arises.

Typically, a managed bean is not used by itself in a Java EE application. However, the concepts defined are very relevant to Java EE and allow you to build other component specifications on it.

Define and Use a Managed Bean

A managed bean is a POJO with a no-args constructor with the class-level annotation `javax.annotation.ManagedBean`:

```
@javax.annotation.ManagedBean("myBean")
public class MyManagedBean {
  //. . .
}
```

This bean can be injected in any other managed component in three different ways:

1. Using `@Resource` annotation as:

   ```
   @Resource
   MyManagedBean bean;
   ```

2. Using `@Inject` annotation as:

   ```
   @Inject
   MyManagedBean bean;
   ```

3. Using the JNDI reference `java:app/ManagedBean/myBean` or `java:module/myBean` where `ManagedBean` is the name of the deployed archive (`.war` in this case):

   ```
   InitialContext ic = new InitialContext();
   MyManagedBean bean = (MyManagedBean)ic.lookup
                         ("java:module/myBean");
   ```

   There is no default name for the managed bean, so it's important to provide a name in order for the JNDI reference to work. EJB and CDI specifications extend this rule and provide default naming rules.

Once the bean is injected, its business methods can be invoked directly. As part of Java EE 6, all EJB and CDI beans are defined as managed beans, and so:

```
@Stateless
public class FooBean {
```

```
  //. . .
}
```

and:

```
@Named
public class BarBean {
  //. . .
}
```

are implicitly managed beans as well.

No other beans in the Java EE platform are currently implicitly defined as managed beans. However, JAX-RS resources can also be defined as EJB and CDI beans, in which case the JAX-RS resources will be implicit managed beans as well. A future version of different component specifications may discuss whether it makes sense to align other Java EE POJO elements with the Managed Beans specification.

Lifecycle Callback

The standard annotations `javax.annotation.PostConstruct` and `javax.annotation.PreDestroy` from JSR 250 can be applied to any methods in the managed bean to perform resource initialization or cleanup:

```
@ManagedBean("myBean")
public class MyManagedBean {
  @PostConstruct
  public void setupResources() {
    //. . .
  }

  @PreDestroy
  public void cleanupResources() {
    //. . .
  }

  public String sayHello() {
    return "Hello " + name;
  }
}
```

The `setupResources` method is where any resources required during business method execution can be acquired, and the `cleanupResources` method is where those resources are closed or released. The lifecycle callback methods are invoked after the no-args constructor.

CHAPTER 3

Servlets

Servlets are defined as JSR 315, and the complete specification can be downloaded from *http://jcp.org/aboutJava/community process/final/jsr315/index.html*.

A servlet is a web component hosted in a servlet container and generates dynamic content. The web clients interact with a servlet using a request/response pattern. The servlet container is responsible for the lifecycle of the servlet, receives requests and sends responses, and performs any other encoding/decoding required as part of that.

Servlets

A servlet is defined using the `@WebServlet` annotation on a POJO, and must extend the `javax.servlet.http.HttpServlet` class.

Here is a sample servlet definition:

```
@WebServlet("/account")
public class AccountServlet
  extends javax.servlet.http.HttpServlet {
  //. . .
}
```

The fully qualified class name is the default servlet name, and may be overridden using the name attribute of the annotation. The servlet may be deployed at multiple URLs:

```
@WebServlet(urlPatterns={"/account", "/accountServlet"})
public class AccountServlet
  extends javax.servlet.http.HttpServlet {
  //. . .
}
```

The @WebInitParam can be used to specify an initialization parameter:

```
@WebServlet(urlPatterns="/account",
            initParams={
                @WebInitParam(name="type", value="checking")
                      }
            )
public class AccountServlet
  extends javax.servlet.http.HttpServlet {
  //. . .
}
```

The Servlet interface has one *doXXX* method to handle each of HTTP GET, POST, PUT, DELETE, HEAD, OPTIONS, and TRACE requests. Typically the developer is concerned with overriding the doGet and doPost methods. The code below shows a servlet handling the GET request:

```
@WebServlet("/account")
public class AccountServlet
  extends javax.servlet.http.HttpServlet {
  @Override
  protected void doGet(
      HttpServletRequest request,
      HttpServletResponse response) {
    //. . .
  }
}
```

In this code:

- The HttpServletRequest and HttpServletResponse capture the request/response with the web client.

- The request parameters, HTTP headers, different parts of the path such as host, port, and context, and much more information is available from `HttpServletRequest`.

The HTTP cookies can be set and retrieved as well. The developer is responsible for populating the `HttpServletResponse`, and the container then transmits the captured HTTP headers and/or the message body to the client.

This code shows how a HTTP GET request received by a servlet displays a simple response to the client:

```
protected void doGet(HttpServletRequest request,
                     HttpServletResponse response) {
    try (PrintWriter out = response.getWriter()) {
    out.println("<html><head>");
    out.println("<title>MyServlet</title>");
    out.println("</head><body>");
    out.println("<h1>My First Servlet</h1>");
    //. . .
    out.println("</body></html>");
    } finally {
    //. . .
    }
}
```

Request parameters may be passed in GET and POST requests. In a GET request, these parameters are passed in the query string as name/value pairs. A sample URL to invoke the servlet explained earlier with request parameters can look like:

```
. . ./account?tx=10
```

In a POST request, the request parameters can also be passed in the posted data that is encoded in the body of the request. In both GET and POST requests, these parameters can be obtained from `HttpServletRequest`:

```
protected void doGet(HttpServletRequest request,
                     HttpServletResponse response) {
    String txValue = request.getParameter("tx");
    //. . .
}
```

Request parameters can differ for each request.

Initialization parameters, also known as init params, may be defined on a servlet to store startup and configuration information. As explained earlier, @WebInitParam is used to specify init params for a servlet:

```java
String type = null;

@Override
public void init(ServletConfig config)
    throws ServletException {
  type = config.getInitParameter("type");
  //. . .
}
```

The default behavior of the servlet's lifecycle call methods may be manipulated by overriding init, service, and destroy methods of the javax.servlet.Servlet interface. Typically, database connections are initialized in init and released in destroy.

A servlet may also be defined using the servlet and servlet-mapping element in the deployment descriptor of the web application, *web.xml*. The AccountServlet may be defined using *web.xml*:

```xml
<?xml version="1.0" encoding="UTF-8"?>
<web-app version="3.0"
  xmlns="http://java.sun.com/xml/ns/javaee"
  xmlns:xsi="http://www.w3.org/2001/XMLSchema-instance"
  xsi:schemaLocation="http://java.sun.com/xml/ns/javaee
  http://java.sun.com/xml/ns/javaee/web-app_3_0.xsd">
  <servlet>
    <servlet-name>AccountServlet</servlet-name>
    <servlet-class>org.sample.AccountServlet
</servlet-class>
  </servlet>
  <servlet-mapping>
    <servlet-name>AccountServlet</servlet-name>
    <url-pattern>/account</url-pattern>
  </servlet-mapping>
</web-app>
```

The annotations cover most of the common cases, so *web.xml* is not required in those cases. But some cases, such as ordering of servlets, can only be done using *web.xml*. If the metadata-complete element in *web.xml* is true, then the annotations in the class are not processed.

The values defined in the deployment descriptor override the values defined using annotations.

A servlet is packaged in a web application in a *.war* file. Multiple servlets may be packaged together, and they all share a *servlet context*. The ServletContext provides detail about the execution environment of the servlets and is used to communicate with the container, for example by reading a resource packaged in the web application, writing to a log file, or dispatching a request.

The ServletContext can be obtained from HttpServletRequest:

```
protected void doGet(HttpServletRequest request,
                     HttpServletResponse response) {
  ServletContext context = request.getServletContext();
  //. . .
}
```

A servlet can send an HTTP cookie, named JSESSIONID, to the client for session tracking. This cookie may be marked as HttpOnly, which ensures that the cookie is not exposed to client-side scripting code, and thus helps mitigate certains kinds of cross-site scripting attacks:

```
SessionCookieConfig config = request.getServletContext().
                             getSessionCookieConfig();
config.setHttpOnly(true);
```

Alternatively, URL rewriting may be used by the servlet as a basis for session tracking. The ServletContext#getSession CookieConfig method returns SessionCookieConfig, which can be used to configure different properties of the cookie.

The HttpSession interface can be used to view and manipulate information about a session such as the session identifier and creation time, and to bind objects to the session. A new session object may be created:

```
protected void doGet(HttpServletRequest request,
                     HttpServletResponse response) {
  HttpSession session = request.getSession(true);
```

```
   //. . .
   }
```

The `session.setAttribute` and `session.getAttribute` methods are used to bind objects to the session.

A servlet may forward a request to another servlet if further processing is required. This can be achieved by dispatching the request to a different resource using `RequestDispatcher`, which can be obtained from `HttpServletRequest.getRequest Dispatcher` or `ServletContext.getRequestDispatcher`. The former can accept a relative path, whereas the latter can accept a path relative to the current context only:

```
protected void doGet(HttpServletRequest request,
                     HttpServletResponse response) {
   request.getRequestDispatcher("bank").
          forward(request, response);
   //. . .
   }
```

In this code, `bank` is another servlet deployed in the same context.

The `ServletContext.getContext` method can be used to obtain `ServletContext` for foreign contexts. It can then be used to obtain a `RequestDispatcher`, which can dispatch requests in that context.

A servlet response may be redirected to another resource by calling the `HttpServletResponse.sendRedirect` method. This sends a temporary redirect response to the client and the client issues a new request to the specified URL. Note that in this case the original request object is not available to the redirected URL. The redirect may also be marginally slower because it entails two requests from the client, whereas `forward` is performed within the container:

```
protected void doGet(HttpServletRequest request,
                     HttpServletResponse response) {
   //. . .
   response.sendRedirect(
          "http://example.com/SomeOtherServlet");
   }
```

Here the response is redirected to the *http://example.com/Some OtherServlet* URL. Note that this URL could be on a different host/port and may be relative or absolute to the container.

In addition to declaring servlets using @WebServlet and *web.xml*, they may also be defined programmatically using ServletContext.addServlet methods. This can be done from the ServletContainerInitializer.onStartup or ServletContext Listener.contextInitialized method. You can read more about this in "Event Listeners" on page 25.

The ServletContainerInitializer.onStartup method is invoked when the application is starting up for the given ServletContext. The addServlet method returns ServletRegis tration.Dynamic, which can then be used to create URL mappings, set security roles, set initialization parameters, and other configuration items:

```
public class MyInitializer
             implements ServletContainerInitializer {
  @Override
  public void onStartup
    (Set<Class<?>> clazz, ServletContext context) {
    ServletRegistration.Dynamic reg =
context.addServlet("MyServlet", "org.example.MyServlet");
    reg.addMapping("/myServlet");
  }
}
```

Servlet Filters

A servlet filter may be used to update the request and response payload and header information from and to the servlet. It is important to realize that filters do not create the response—they only modify or adapt the requests and responses. Authentication, logging, data compression, and encryption are some typical use cases for filters. The filters are packaged along with a servlet and act upon the dynamic or static content.

Filters can be associated with a servlet or with a group of servlets and static content by specifying a URL pattern. A filter is defined using @WebFilter annotation:

```
@WebFilter("/*")
public class LoggingFilter
  implements javax.servlet.Filter {
  public void doFilter(HttpServletRequest request,
                       HttpServletResponse response) {
    //. . .
  }
}
```

In the code shown, the LoggingFilter is applied to all the servlets and static content pages in the web application.

The @WebInitParam may be used to specify initialization parameters here as well.

A filter and the target servlet always execute in the same invocation thread. Multiple filters may be arranged in a filter chain.

A filter may also be defined using <filter> and <filter-mapping> elements in the deployment descriptor:

```
<filter>
  <filter-name>LoggingFilter</filter-name>
  <filter-class>org.sample.LoggingFilter</filter-class>
</filter>
    . . .
<filter-mapping>
  <filter-name>LoggingFilter</filter-name>
  <url-pattern>/*</url-pattern>
</filter-mapping>
```

In addition to declaring filters using @WebFilter and *web.xml*, they may also be defined programmatically using ServletContext.addFilter methods. This can be done from the ServletContainerInitializer.onStartup method or the ServletContextListener.contextInitialized method. The addFilter method returns ServletRegistration.Dynamic, which can then be used to add mapping for URL patterns, set initialization parameters, and other configuration items:

```
public class MyInitializer
  implements ServletContainerInitializer {
```

```
    public void onStartup
      (Set<Class<?>> clazz, ServletContext context) {
      FilterRegistration.Dynamic reg =
  context.addServlet("LoggingFilter",
                      "org.example.LoggingFilter");
      reg.addMappingForUrlPatterns(null, false, "/");
    }
  }
```

Event Listeners

Event listeners provide lifecycle callback events for `ServletContext`, `HttpSession`, and `ServletRequest` objects. These listeners are classes that implement an interface that supports event notifications for state changes in these objects. Each class is annotated with `@WebListener`, declared in *web.xml*, or registered via one of the `ServletContext.addListener` methods. A typical example of these listeners is where an additional servlet is registered programmatically without an explicit need for the programmer to do so, or a database connection is initialized and restored back at the application level.

There may be multiple listener classes listening to each event type, and they may be specified in the order in which the container invokes the listener beans for each event type. The listeners are notified in the reverse order during application shutdown.

Servlet context listeners listen to the events from resources in that context:

```
@WebListener
public class MyContextListener
              implements ServletContextListener {

  @Override
  public void contextInitialized(ServletContextEvent sce) {
    ServletContext context = sce.getServletContext();
    //. . .
  }

  @Override
  public void contextDestroyed(ServletContextEvent sce) {
```

```
    //. . .
  }
}
```

The ServletContextAttributeListener is used to listen for attribute changes in the context:

```
public class MyServletContextAttributeListener
             implements ServletContextAttributeListener {

  @Override
  public void attributeAdded
  (ServletContextAttributeEvent event) {
    //. . . event.getName();
    //. . . event.getValue();
  }

  @Override
  public void attributeRemoved(
             ServletContextAttributeEvent event) {
    //. . .
  }

  @Override
  public void attributeReplaced(
             ServletContextAttributeEvent event) {
    //. . .
  }

}
```

The HttpSessionListener listens to events from resources in
that session:

```
@WebListener
public class MySessionListener
             implements HttpSessionListener {

  @Override
  public void sessionCreated(HttpSessionEvent hse) {
    HttpSession session = hse.getSession();
    //. . .
  }

  @Override
  public void sessionDestroyed(HttpSessionEvent hse) {
    //. . .
```

```
    }
  }
```

The HttpSessionActivationListener is used to listen for events when the session is passivated or activated:

```
public class MyHttpSessionActivationListener
            implements HttpSessionActivationListener {

  @Override
  public void sessionWillPassivate(HttpSessionEvent hse) {
    // ... hse.getSession();
  }

  @Override
  public void sessionDidActivate(HttpSessionEvent hse) {
    // ...
  }
}
```

The HttpSessionAttributeListener is used to listen for attribute changes in the session:

```
public class MyHttpSessionAttributeListener
            implements HttpSessionAttributeListener {

  @Override
  public void attributeAdded(
    HttpSessionBindingEvent event) {
    HttpSession session = event.getSession();
    //. . . event.getName();
    //. . . event.getValue();
  }

  @Override
  public void attributeRemoved(
      HttpSessionBindingEvent event) {
    //. . .
  }

  @Override
  public void attributeReplaced(
      HttpSessionBindingEvent event) {
    //. . .
  }
}
```

The HttpSessionBindingListener is used to listen to events when an object is bound to or unbound from a session:

```java
public class MyHttpSessionBindingListener
               implements HttpSessionBindingListener {

  @Override
  public void valueBound(HttpSessionBindingEvent event) {
    HttpSession session = event.getSession();
    //. . . event.getName();
    //. . . event.getValue();
  }

  @Override
  public void valueUnbound(HttpSessionBindingEvent event)
  {
    //. . .
  }
}
```

The ServletRequestListener listens to the events from resources in that request:

```java
@WebListener
public class MyRequestListener
               implements ServletRequestListener {
  @Override
  public void requestDestroyed(ServletRequestEvent sre) {
    ServletRequest request = sre.getServletRequest();
    //. . .
  }

  @Override
  public void requestInitialized(ServletRequestEvent sre) {
    //. . .
  }
}
```

The ServletRequestAttributeListener is used to listen for attribute changes in the request.

There is also AsyncListener, which is used to manage async events such as completed, timed out, or an error.

In addition to declaring listeners using @WebListener and *web.xml*, they may also be defined programmatically using ServletContext.addListener methods. This can be done from the `ServletContainerInitializer.onStartup` or `ServletContext Listener.contextInitialized` method.

The `ServletContainerInitializer.onStartup` method is invoked when the application is starting up for the given `ServletContext`:

```
public class MyInitializer
              implements ServletContainerInitializer {
  public void onStartup(
    Set<Class<?>> clazz, ServletContext context) {
    context.addListener("org.example.MyContextListener");
  }
}
```

Asynchronous Support

Server resources are valuable and should be used conservatively. Consider a servlet that has to wait for a JDBC connection to be available from the pool, receiving a JMS message or reading a resource from the file system. Waiting for a "long-running" process to return completely blocks the thread—waiting, sitting, and doing nothing—not an optimal usage of your server resources. This is where the server can be asynchronously processed such that the control (or thread) is returned back to the container to perform other tasks while waiting for the long-running process to complete. The request processing continues in the same thread after the response from the long-running process is returned, or may be dispatched to a new resource from within the long-running process. A typical use case for long-running process is a chat application.

The asynchronous behavior needs to be explicitly enabled on a servlet. This is achieved by adding the `asyncSupported` attribute on `@WebServlet`:

```
@WebServlet(urlPatterns="/async", asyncSupported=true)
public class MyAsyncServlet extends HttpServlet {
  //. . .
}
```

It can also be enabled by specifying the `<async-supported>` element to true in *web.xml* or calling `ServletRegistration.setAsyncSupported(true)` during programmatic registration.

The asynchronous processing can then be started in a separate thread using the `startAsync` method on the request. This method returns `AsyncContext`, which represents the execution context of the asynchronous request. The asynchronous request can then be completed by calling `AsyncContext.complete` (explicit) or dispatching to another resource (implicit). The container completes the invocation of the asynchronous request in the latter case.

Let's say the long-running process is implemented:

```
class MyAsyncService implements Runnable {
  AsyncContext ac;

  public MyAsyncService(AsyncContext ac) {
    this.ac = ac;
  }

  @Override
  public void run() {
    //. . .
    ac.complete();
  }
}
```

This service may be invoked from the `doGet` method:

```
@Override
protected void doGet(HttpServletRequest request,
                     HttpServletResponse response) {
  AsyncContext ac = request.startAsync();
  ac.addListener(new AsyncListener() {
    public void onComplete(AsyncEvent event)
        throws IOException {
      //. . .
    }

    public void onTimeout(AsyncEvent event)
        throws IOException {
      //. . .
    }
    //. . .
```

```
    });

    ScheduledThreadPoolExexcutor executor =
        new ScheduledThreadPoolExexcutor(10);
    executor.execut(new MyAsyncService(ac));
}
```

In this code, the request is put into asynchronous mode. `AsyncListener` is registered to listen for events when the request processing is complete, timed out, and other required behavior. The long-running service is invoked in a separate thread and calls `AsyncContext.complete`, signalling the completion of request processing.

A request may be dispatched from an asynchronous servlet to synchronous, but the other way around is illegal.

The asynchronous behavior is available in the servlet filter as well.

Web Fragments

A web fragment is part or all of the *web.xml* included in a library or framework JAR's *META-INF* directory. If this framework is bundled in the *WEB-INF/lib* directory, the container will pick up and configure the framework without requiring the developer to do it explicitly.

It can include almost all of the elements that can be specified in *web.xml*. However, the top-level element must be `web-fragment` and the corresponding *file* must be called *web-fragment.xml*. This allows logical partitioning of the web application:

```
<web-fragment>
  <filter>
    <filter-name>MyFilter</filter-name>
    <filter-class>org.example.MyFilter</filter-class>
    <init-param>
      <param-name>myInitParam</param-name>
      <param-value>...</param-value>
    </init-param>
  </filter>
```

```
<filter-mapping>
  <filter-name>MyFilter</filter-name>
  <url-pattern>/*</url-pattern>
</filter-mapping>
</web-fragment>
```

The developer can specify the order in which the resources specified in *web.xml* and *web-fragment.xml* need to be loaded. The `<absolute-ordering>` element in *web.xml* is used to specify the exact order in which the resources should be loaded, and the `<ordering>` element within *web-fragment.xml* is used to specify relative ordering. The two orders are mutually exclusive, and absolute ordering overrides relative.

The absolute ordering contains one or more `<name>` elements specifying the name of the resources and the order in which they need to be loaded. Specifying `<others/>` allows for the other resources not named in the ordering to be loaded:

```
<web-app>
  <name>MyApp</name>
  <absolute-ordering>
    <name>MyServlet</name>
    <name>MyFilter</name>
  </absolute-ordering>
</web-app>
```

In this code, the resources specified in *web.xml* are loaded first and followed by `MyServlet` and `MyFilter`.

Zero or one `<before>` and `<after>` elements in `<ordering>` are used to specify the resources that need to be loaded before and after the resource named in the `web-fragment` is loaded:

```
<web-fragment>
  <name>MyFilter</name>
  <ordering>
    <after>MyServlet</after>
  </ordering>
</web-fragment>
```

This code will require the container to load the resource `MyFilter` after the resource `MyServlet` (defined elsewhere) is loaded.

If *web.xml* has `metadata-complete` set to true, then the *web-fragment.xml* is not processed. The *web.xml* has the highest precedence when resolving conflicts between *web.xml* and *web-fragment.xml*.

If a *web-fragment.xml* does not have an `<ordering>` element and *web.xml* does not have an `<absolute-ordering>` element, the resources are assumed to not have any ordering dependency.

Security

Servlets are typically accessed over the Internet, and thus having a security requirement is common. The servlet security model, including roles, access control, and authentication requirements, can be specified using annotations or in *web.xml*.

`@ServletSecurity` is used to specify security constraints on the servlet implementation class for all methods or a specific *doXXX* method. The container will enforce that the corresponding *doXXX* messages can be invoked by users in the specified roles:

```
@WebServlet("/account")
@ServletSecurity(
  value=@HttpConstraint(rolesAllowed = {"R1"}),
  httpMethodConstraints={
    @HttpMethodConstraint(value="GET",
                          rolesAllowed="R2"),
    @HttpMethodConstraint(value="POST",
                          rolesAllowed={"R3", "R4"})
  }
)
public class AccountServlet
              extends javax.servlet.http.HttpServlet {
  //. . .
}
```

In this code, `@HttpMethodConstraint` is used to specify that the `doGet` method can be invoked by users in the `R2` role, and the `doPost` method can be invoked by users in the `R3` and `R4` roles. The `@HttpConstraint` specifies that all other methods can be invoked by users in the role R1. The roles are mapped to security principals or groups in the container.

The security constraints can also be specified using the `<security-constraint>` element in *web.xml*. Within it, a `<web-resource-collection>` element is used to specify constraints on HTTP operations and web resources, `<auth-constraint>` is used to specify the roles permitted to access the resource, and `<user-data-constraint>` indicates how data between the client and server should be protected by the subelement `<transport-guarantee>`:

```
<security-constraint>
  <web-resource-collection>
    <url-pattern>/account/*</url-pattern>
    <http-method>GET</http-method>
  </web-resource-collection>

  <auth-constraint>
    <role-name>manager</role-name>
  </auth-constraint>

  <user-data-constraint>
    <transport-guarantee>INTEGRITY</transport-guarantee>
  </user-data-constraint>
</security-constraint>
```

This deployment descriptor requires that the **doGet** method can only be accessed by a user in **manager** role with a requirement for content integrity.

@RolesAllowed, @DenyAll, @PermitAll, and @Transport Protected provide an alternative set of annotations to specify security roles on a particular resource or method of the resource:

```
@RolesAllowed("R2")
protected void doGet(HttpServletRequest request,
HttpServletResponse response) {
  //. . .
}
```

If an annotation is specified on both the class and the method level, the one specified on the method overrides the one specified on the class.

At most, one of @RolesAllowed, @DenyAll, or @PermitAll may be specified on a target. The @TransportProtected annotation may occur in combination with either the @RolesAllowed or @PermitAll annotations.

The servlets can be configured for HTTP Basic, HTTP Digest, HTTPS Client, and form-based authentication:

```
<form method="POST" action="j_security_check">
    <input type="text" name="j_username">
    <input type="password" name="j_password">
    <input type="button" value="submit">
</form>
```

This code shows how form-based authentication can be achieved. The login form must contain fields for entering a username and a password. These fields must be named j_user name and j_password, respectively. The action of the form is always j_security_check.

The HttpServletRequest also provides programmatic security with the login, logout, and authenticate methods.

The login method validates the provided username and password in the password validation realm (specific to a container) configured for the ServletContext. This ensures that getUser Principal, getRemoteUser, and getAuthType methods return valid values. The login method can be used as a replacement for form-based login.

The authenticate method uses the container login mechanism configured for the ServletContext to authenticate the user making this request.

Resource Packaging

Resources bundled in the *.war* file are accessible using Servlet Context.getResource and .getResourceAsStream methods. The resource path is specified as String with a leading "/." This path is resolved relative to the root of the context or relative to the *META-INF/resources* directory of the JAR files bundled in the *WEB-INF/lib* directory:

```
myApplication.war
  WEB-INF
    lib
      library.jar
```

library.jar has the following structure:

```
library.jar
  MyClass1.class
  MyClass2.class
  stylesheets
    common.css
  images
    header.png
    footer.png
```

If the resources bundled in the *stylesheets* and *images* directories need to be accessed in the servlet, they need to be manually extracted in the root of the web application. The library can package the resources in the *META-INF/resources* directory:

```
library.jar
  MyClass1.class
  MyClass2.class
  META-INF
    resources
      stylesheets
        common.css
      images
        header.png
        footer.png
```

In this case, the resources need not be extracted to the root of the application and can be accessed directly instead. This allows resources from third-party JARs bundled in *META-INF/ resources* to be accessed directly instead of extracting them manually.

Resources are always looked for in the root of the application before scanning through the JARs bundled in the *WEB-INF/ lib* directory. The order of scanning JAR files in the *WEB-INF/lib* directory is undefined.

Error Mapping

An HTTP error code or an exception thrown by a serlvet can be mapped to a resource bundled with the application to customize the appearance of content when a servlet generates an error. This allows fine-grained mapping of errors from your web application to custom pages. These pages are defined using `<error-page>`:

```
<error-page>
  <error-code>404</error-code>
  <location>/error-404.jsp</location>
</error-page>
```

Adding the above fragment to *web.xml* will display the `/error-404.jsp` page to the client if a nonexisting resource is accessed. This mapping can be easily done for other HTTP status codes as well by adding other `<error-page>` elements.

The `<exception-type>` element is used to map an exception thrown by a servlet to a resource in the web application:

```
<error-page>
  <exception-type>org.example.MyException</exception-type>
  <location>/error.jsp</location>
</error-page>
```

Adding the above fragment to *web.xml* will display the `/error.jsp` page to the client if the servlet throws the `org.example.MyException` exception. This mapping can be easily done for other exceptions as well by adding other `<error-page>` elements.

The `<error-page>` declaration must be unique for each class name and HTTP status code.

Handling Multipart Requests

`@MultipartConfig` may be specified on a servlet indicating that it expects a request of type `multipart/form-data`. The `HttpServletRequest.getParts` and `.getPart` methods then make the various parts of the multipart request available:

```
@WebServlet(urlPatterns = {"/FileUploadServlet"})
@MultipartConfig(location="/tmp")
public class FileUploadServlet extends HttpServlet {

  @Override
  protected void doPost(HttpServletRequest request,
                        HttpServletResponse response)
      throws ServletException, IOException {
    for (Part part : request.getParts()) {
      part.write("myFile");
    }
  }
}
```

In this code:

- @MultipartConfig is specified on the class indicating the
  doPost method will receive a request of type multipart/
  form-data

- location attribute is used to specify the directory location
  where the files are stored

- getParts method provides a Collection of parts for this
  multipart request

- part.write is used to write this uploaded part to disk

This servlet can be invoked from a JSP page:

```
<form action="FileUploadServlet"
      enctype="multipart/form-data"
      method="POST">
    <input type="file" name="myFile"><br>
    <input type="Submit" value="Upload File"><br>
</form>
```

In this code, the form is POSTed to FileUploadServlet with encoding multipart/form-data.

CHAPTER 4

Java Persistence API

The Java Persistence API (JPA) is defined as JSR 317, and the complete specification can be downloaded from *http://jcp.org/ aboutJava/communityprocess/final/jsr317/index.html*.

JPA defines an API for the management of persistence and object/relational mapping using a Java domain model.

A database table, typically with multiple columns, stores the persistent state of an application. Multiple rows are stored in the database table to capture different states. A single column or combination of columns may define the uniqueness of each row using primary key constraint. Typically, an application accesses and stores data to multiple tables. These tables generally have relationships defined among them using foreign key constraint.

JPA defines a standard mapping between a database table and a POJO. It defines syntax to capture primary and foreign key constraints and how these rows can be created, read, updated, and deleted using these POJOs. Transactions, caching, validation, and other similar capabilities required by an application accessing a database are also defined by JPA.

This chapter will discuss the key concepts of JPA.

Entities

A POJO with a no-arg public constructor is used to define the mapping with one or more relational database tables. Each such class is annotated with @Entity, and the instance variables that follow JavaBeans-style properties represent the persistent state of the entity. The mapping between the table column and the field name is derived following reasonable defaults and can be overridden by annotations. For example, the table name is the same as the class name, and the column names are the same as the persistent field names.

Here is a simple entity definition describing a student:

```
@Entity
public class Student implements Serializable {
  @Id
  private int id;
  private String name;
  private String grade;
  @Embedded
  private Address address;

  @ElementCollection
  @CollectionTable("StudentCourse")
  List<Course> courses;

  //. . .
}
```

A few things to observe in this code:

- This class has a no-arg constructor by default, as no other constructors are defined.

- The entity's persistent state is defined by four fields; the identity is defined by the field **id** and is annotated with **@Id**. A composite primary key may also be defined where the primary key corresponds to one or more fields of the entity class.

- The class implements a **Serializable** interface, and that allows it to be passed by value through a remote interface.

- `Address` is a POJO class that does not have a persistent identity of its own and exclusively belongs to the `Student` class. This class is called as an *embeddable class* and is identified by `@Embedded` on the field in the entity class and annotated with `@Embeddable` in the class definition:

    ```
    @Embeddable
    public class Address {
      private String street;
      private String city;
      private String zip;
      //. . .
    }
    ```

    This allows the database structure to be more naturally mapped in Java.

- The `@ElementCollection` annotation signifies that a student's courses are listed in a different table. By default, the table name is derived by combining the name of the owning class, the string "_," and the field name. `@CollectionTable` can be used to override the default name of the table, and `@AtttributeOverrides` can be used to override the default column names. `@ElementCollection` can also be applied to an embeddable class.

The persistent fields or properties of an entity may be of the following types: Java primitive types, `java.lang.String`, `java.math.BigInteger`, `java.math.BigDecimal`, `java.util.Date`, `java.util.Calendar`, `java.sql.Date`, `java.sql.Time`, `java.sql.Timestamp`, `byte[]`, `Byte[]`, `char[]`, `Character[]`, enums and other Java serializable types, entity types, collections of entity types, embeddable classes, and collections of basic and embeddable classes. The `@Temporal` annotation may be specified on fields of type `java.util.Date` and `java.util.Calendar` to specify the temporal type of the field.

An entity may inherit from a superclass that provides persistent entity state and mapping information, but which itself may or may not be an entity. An entity superclass is abstract and cannot be directly instantiated but can be used to create polymorphic queries.

The @Inheritance and @Discriminator annotations are used to specify the inheritance from an entity superclass. The @Mapped Superclass annotation is used to designate a nonentity superclass and captures state and mapping information that is common to multiple entity classes. Such a class has no separate table defined for it, so the mappings will only apply to its subclasses. An entity may inherit from a superclass that provides inheritance of behavior only. Such a class does not contain any persistent state.

The relationships between different entities are defined using @OneToOne, @OneToMany, @ManyToOne, and @ManyToMany annotation on the corresponding field of the referencing entity. A unidirectional relationship requires the owning side to specify the annotation. A bidirectional relationship also requires the nonowning side to refer to its owning side by use of the map pedBy element of the OneToOne, OneToMany, or ManyToMany annotation.

The FetchType.EAGER annotation may be specified on an entity to eagerly load the data from the database. The Fetch Type.LAZY annotation may be specified as a hint that the data should be fetched lazily when it is first accessed.

The entities may display a collection of elements and entity relationships as java.util.Map collections. The map key may be the primary key or a persistent field or property of the entity. @MapKey is used to specify the key for the association. For example, all the Courses by a Student can be modeled as:

```
public class Student {
  @MapKey
  private Map<Integer, Course> courses;
  //. . .
}
```

In this code, specifying @MapKey on the Map indicates that the map key is the primary key as well.

The map key can be a basic type, an embeddable class, or an entity. If a persistent field or property other than the primary key is used as a map key, then it is expected to have a uniqueness constraint associated with it. In this case, `@MapKey` `Column` is used to specify the mapping for the key column of the map:

```
public class Student {
  @MapKeyColumn(name="year")
  private Map<Integer, Course> courses;
  //. . .
}
```

In this code, `Map` represents all the `Course`s taken by a `Student` in a year. If the `name` element is not specified, it defaults to the concatenation of the following: the name of the referencing relationship field or property, "_," and "KEY." In this case, the default name will be `COURSES_KEY`.

`@MapKeyClass` can be used to specify the map key for the association. If the value is an entity, then `@OneToMany` and `@ManyTo` `Many` may be used to specify the mapping:

```
public class Student {
  @OneToMany
  @MapKeyClass(PhoneType.class)
  private Map<PhoneType, Phone> phones;
  //. . .
}
```

`@MapKeyClass` and `@MapKey` are mutually exclusive.

If the value is a basic type or embeddable class, then `@Element` `Collection` is used to specify the mapping.

Persistence Unit, Persistence Context, and Entity Manager

An entity is managed within a *persistence context*. Each entity has a unique instance for any persistent entity identity within the context. Within the persistence context, the entity instances and their lifecycles are managed by the *entity manager*. The entity manager may be *container-managed* or *application-managed*.

A container-managed entity manager is obtained by the application directly through dependency injection or from JNDI:

```
@PersistenceContext
EntityManager em;
```

The persistence context is propagated across multiple transactions for a container-managed entity manager, and the container is responsible for managing the lifecycle of the entity manager.

An application-managed entity manager is obtained by the application from an entity manager factory:

```
@PersistenceUnit
EntityManagerFactory emf;
//. . .
EntityManager em = emf.createEntityManager();
```

A new isolated persistence context is created when a new entity manager is requested, and the application is responsible for managing the lifecycle of the entity manager.

A container-managed entity manager is typically used in a Java EE environment. The application-managed entity manager is typically used in a Java SE environment and will not be discussed here.

An entity manager and persistence context are not required to be threadsafe. This requires an entity manager to be obtained from an entity manager factory in Java EE components that are not required to be threadsafe, such as servlets.

The entity managers, together with their configuration information, the set of entities managed by the entity managers, and metadata that specifies mapping of the classes to the database, are packaged together as a *persistence unit*. A persistence unit is defined by a *persistence.xml* and is contained within an *ejb-jar*, *.war*, *.ear*, or application-client *JAR*. Multiple persistence units may be defined within a *persistence.xml*.

A sample *persistence.xml* for the entity can be defined:

```
<?xml version="1.0" encoding="UTF-8"?>
<persistence version="2.0"
```

```
    xmlns="http://java.sun.com/xml/ns/persistence"
    xmlns:xsi="http://www.w3.org/2001/XMLSchema-instance"
    xsi:schemaLocation=
        "http://java.sun.com/xml/ns/persistence
  http://java.sun.com/xml/ns/persistence/persistence_2_0.xsd">
    <persistence-unit name="MyPU" transaction-type="JTA">
      <provider>
          org.eclipse.persistence.jpa.PersistenceProvider
      </provider>
          <jta-data-source>jdbc/sample</jta-data-source>
      <exclude-unlisted-classes>
          false
      </exclude-unlisted-classes>
      <properties>
        <property name="eclipselink.ddl-generation"
        value="create-tables"/>
      </properties>
    </persistence-unit>
  </persistence>
```

In this code:

- Persistence unit's name is `"MyPU"`.

- `transaction-type` attribute's value of JTA signifies that a JTA data source is provided.

- `<provider>` element is optional and specifies the name of the persistence provider.

- `jta-data-source` element defines the global JNDI name of the JTA data source defined in the container. In a Java EE environment, this ensures that all the database configuration information, such as host, port, username, and password, are specified in the container, and just the JTA data source name is used in the application.

- Explicit list of entity classes to be managed can be specified using multiple `class` elements, or all the entities may be included (as above) by specifying the `exclude-unlisted-classes` element.

- `properties` element is used to specify both standard and vendor-specific properties. In this case, the `eclipselink.ddl-generation` property is specified and the property value indicates to generate the tables using the

mappings defined in the entity class. The following standard properties may be specified: `javax.persistence`
`.jdbc.driver`, `javax.persistence.jdbc.url`, `javax.persis`
`tence.jdbc.user`, `javax.persistence.jdbc.password`.

By default, a container-managed persistence context is scoped to a single transaction, and entities are detached at the end of a transaction. For stateful session beans, the persistence context may be marked to span multiple transactions and is called *extended persistence context*. The entities stay managed across multiple transactions in this case. An extended persistence context can be created:

```
@PersistenceContext(type=PersistenceContextType.EXTENDED)
EntityManager em;
```

Create, Read, Update, and Delete Entities

An entity goes through create, read, update, and delete (CRUD) operations during its lifecycle. A create operation means a new entity is created and persisted in the database. A read operation means querying for an entity from the database based upon a selection criteria. An update operation means updating the state of an existing entity in the database. And a delete operation means removing an entity from the database. Typically, an entity is created once, read and updated a few times, and deleted once.

The JPA specification allows the following ways to perform the CRUD operations:

Java Persistence Query Language (JPQL)
> The Java Persistence Query Language is a string-based typed query language used to define queries over entities and their persistent state. The query language uses an SQL-like syntax and uses the abstract persistence schema of entities as its data model. This portable query language syntax is translated into SQL queries that are executed over the database schema where the entities are mapped. The `EntityManager.createNamedXXX` methods are used to

create the JPQL statements. The query statements can be used to select, update, or delete rows from the database.

Criteria API

The Criteria API is an object-based, type-safe API and operates on a metamodel of the entities. Typically, the static metamodel classes are generated using an annotation processor, and model the persistent state and relationships of the entities. The `javax.persistence.criteria` and `javax.persistence.metamodel` APIs are used to create the strongly typed queries. The Criteria API allows only querying the entities.

Native SQL statement

Create a native SQL query specific to a database. `@SQLResultSetMapping` is used to specify the mapping of the result of a native SQL query. The `EntityManager.crea teNativeXXX` methods are used to create native queries.

A new entity can be persisted in the database using an entity manager:

```
Student student = new Student();
student.setId(1234);
//. . .
em.persist(student);
```

In this code, em is an entity manager obtained as explained earlier. The entity is persisted to the database at transaction commit.

A simple JPQL statement to query all the Student entities and retrieve the results looks like:

```
em.createNamedQuery("SELECT s FROM Student s").
    getResultList();
```

`@NamedQuery` and `@NamedQueries` are used to define a mapping between a static JPQL query statement and a symbolic name. This follows the "Don't Repeat Yourself" design pattern and allows you to centralize the JPQL statements:

```
@NamedQuery(
  name="findStudent"
  value="SELECT s FROM Student s WHERE p.grade = :grade")
```

```
//. . .
Query query = em.createNamedQuery("findStudent");
List<Student> list = (List<Student>)query
                        .setParameter("grade", "4")
                        .getResultList();
```

This code will query the database for all the students in grade 4 and return the result as List<Student>.

The usual WHERE, GROUP BY, HAVING, and ORDER BY clauses may be specified in the JPQL statements to restrict the results returned by the query. Other SQL keywords such as JOIN and DISTINCT and functions like ABS, MIN, SIZE, SUM, and TRIM are also permitted. The KEY, VALUE, and ENTRY operators may be applied where map-valued associations or collections are returned.

The return type of the query result list may be specified:

```
TypedQuery<Student> query = em.createNamedQuery(
                                "findStudent",
                                Student.class);
List<Student> list = query
                        .setParameter("grade", "4")
                        .getResultList();
```

Typically a persistence provider will precompile the static named queries. A dynamic JPQL query may be defined by directly passing the query string to the corresponding **create Query** methods:

```
TypedQuery<Student> query = em.createQuery(
                            "SELECT s FROM Student s",
                            Student.class);
```

The query string is dynamically constructed in this case.

JPA also allows dynamic queries to be constructed using a type-safe Criteria API. Here is sample code that explains how to use the Criteria API to query the list of Students:

```
CriteriaBuilder builder = em.getCriteriaBuilder();
CriteriaQuery criteria = builder.createQuery
                            (Student.class);

Root<Student> root = criteria.from(Student.class);
criteria.select(root);
```

```
TypedQuery<Student> query = em.createQuery(criteria);
List<Student> list = query.getResultList();
```

The static @NamedQuery may be more appropriate for simple use cases. In a complex query where SELECT, FROM, WHERE, and other clauses are defined at runtime, the dynamic JPQL may be more error prone, typically because of string concatenation. The type-safe Criteria API offers a more robust way of dealing with such queries. All the clauses can be easily specified in a type-safe manner, providing the advantages of compile-time validation of queries.

The JPA2 metamodel classes capture the metamodel of the persistent state and relationships of the managed classes of a persistence unit. This abstract persistence schema is then used to author the type-safe queries using the Criteria API. The canonical metamodel classes can be generated statically using an annotation processor following the rules defined by the specification. The good thing is that no extra configuration is required to generate these metamodel classes.

To update an existing entity, you need to first find it, change the fields, and call the EntityManager.merge method:

```
Student student = (Student)query
                        .setParameter("id", "1234")
                        .getSingleResult();
//. . .
student.setGrade("5");
em.merge(student);
```

The entity may be updated using JPQL:

```
Query query = em.createQuery("UPDATE Student s"
+ "SET s.grade = :grade WHERE s.id = :id");
query.setParameter("grade", "5");
query.setParameter("id", "1234");
query.executeUpdate();
```

To remove an existing entity, you need to find it and then call the EntityManager.remove method:

```
Student student = em.find(Student.class, 1234);
em.remove(student);
```

The entity may be deleted using JPQL:

```
Query query = em.createQuery("DELETE FROM Student s"
+ "WHERE s.id = :id");
query.setParameter("id", "1234");
query.executeUpdate();
```

Removing an entity removes the corresponding record from the underlying datastore as well.

Validating the Entities

Bean Validation 1.0 is a new specification in the Java EE 6 platform that allows you to specify validation metadata on JavaBeans. For JPA, all managed classes (entities, managed superclasses, and embeddable classes) may be configured to include Bean Validation constraints. These constraints are then enforced when the entity is persisted, updated, or removed in the database. Bean Validation has some predefined constraints like @Min, @Max, @Pattern, and @Size. A custom constraint can be easily defined by using the mechanisms defined in the Bean Validation specification and explained in this book.

The automatic validation is achieved by delegating validating to the Bean Validation implementation in the pre-persist, pre-update, and pre-remove lifecycle callback methods. Alternatively, the validation can also be achieved by the application by calling the Validator.validate method upon an instance of a managed class. The lifecycle event validation only occurs when a Bean Validation provider exists in the runtime.

The Student entity with validation constraints can be defined as:

```
@Entity
public class Student implements Serializable {
  @NotNull
  @Id private int id;

  @Size(max=30)
  private String name;
```

```
@Size(min=2, max=5)
private String grade;

//. . .
}
```

This ensures that the id field is never null, the size of the name field is at most 30 characters with a default minimum of 0, and the size of the grade field is a minimum of 2 characters and a maximum of 5. With these constraints, attempting to add the following Student to the database will throw a ConstraintViolationException, as the grade field must be at least 2 characters long:

```
Student student = new Student();
student.setId(1234);
student.setName("Joe Smith");
student.setGrade("1");
em.persist(student);
```

Embeddable attributes are validated only if the Valid annotation has been specified on them. So the updated Address class will look like:

```
@Embeddable
@Valid
public class Address {
  @Size(max=20)
  private String street;

  @Size(max=20)
  private String city;

  @Size(max=20)
  private String zip;
  //. . .
}
```

By default, the validation of entity beans is automatically turned on. The behavior can be controlled using the validation-mode element in the *persistence.xml* file. This element can take the values AUTO, CALLBACK, or NONE. If the entity manager is created using Persistence.createEntityManager, the validation mode can be specified using the javax.persistence.validation.mode property.

By default, all the entities in a web application are in the `Default` validation group. This ensures that constraints are enforced when a new entity is inserted or updated, while no validation takes place by default if an entity is deleted. This default behavior can be overridden by specifying the target groups using the following validation properties in *persistence.xml*:

- `javax.persistence.validation.group.pre-persist`
- `javax.persistence.validation.group.pre-update`
- `javax.persistence.validation.group.pre-remove`

A new validation group can be defined by declaring a new interface:

```
public interface MyGroup { }
```

A field in the `Student` entity can be targeted to this validation group:

```
@Entity
public class Student implements Serializable {
  @Id @NotNull int id;

  @AssertTrue(groups=MyGroup.class)
  private boolean canBeDeleted;

}
```

And *persistence.xml* needs to have the following property defined:

```
//. . .
<property
   name="javax.persistence.validation.group.pre-remove"
   value="org.sample.MyGroup"/>
```

Transactions and Locking

The `EntityManager.persist`, `.merge`, `.remove`, and `.refresh` methods must be invoked within a transaction context when an entity manager with a transaction-scoped persistence context is used. The transactions are controlled either through JTA or through the use of the resource-local `EntityTransaction` API. A container-managed entity manager must use JTA and is the typical way of having transactional behavior in a Java EE container. A resource-local entity manager is typically used in a Java SE environment.

A transaction for a JTA entity manager is started and committed external to the entity manager:

```
@Stateless
public class StudentSessionBean {
  @PersistenceContext
  EntityManager em;

  public void addStudent(Student student) {
    em.persist(student);
  }
}
```

In this Enterprise JavaBean, a JTA transaction is started before the `addStudent` method and committed after the method is completed. The transaction is automatically rolled back if an exception is thrown in the method.

The resource-local `EntityTransaction` API can be used:

```
EntityManagerFactory emf =
    Persistence.createEntityManagerFactory("student");
em.getTransaction().begin();
Student student = new Student();
//. . .
em.persist(student);
em.getTransaction().commit();
em.close();
emf.close();
```

The transaction may be rolled back using the `EntityTransaction.rollback` method.

In addition to transactions, an entity may be locked when the transaction is active. By default, *optimistic concurrency control* is assumed. The `@Version` attribute on an entity's field is used by the persistence provider to perform optimistic locking. A *pessimistic lock* is configured using `PessimisticLockScope` and `LockModeType` enums. In addition, the `javax.persistence`

`.lock.scope` and `javax.persistence.lock.timeout` properties may be used to configure pessimistic locking.

Caching

JPA provides two levels of caching. The entities are cached by the entity manager at the first level in the persistence context. The entity manager guarantees that within a single persistence context, for any particular database row, there will only be one object instance. However, the same entity could be managed in another transaction, so appropriate locking should be used as explained above.

Second-level caching by the persistence provider can be enabled by the value of the `shared-cache-mode` element in *persistence.xml*. This element can have the values defined in Table 4-1.

Table 4-1. shared-cache-mode values in persistence.xml

Value	Description
ALL	All entities and entity-related state are cached.
NONE	No entities or entity-related state is cached.
ENABLE_SELECTIVE	Only cache entities marked with @Cacheable(true).
DISABLE_SELECTIVE	Only cache entities that are not marked @Cacheable(false).
UNSPECIFIED	Persistence provider specific defaults apply.

The exact value can be specified:

```
<shared-cache-element>ALL</shared-cache-element>
```

This allows entity state to be shared across multiple persistence contexts.

The `Cache` interface can be used to interface with the second-level cache as well. This interface can be obtained from `EntityManagerFactory`. It can be used to check whether a particular entity exists in the cache or invalidate a particular entity, an entire class, or the entire cache:

```
@PersistenceUnit
EntityMangagerFactory emf;

public void myMethod() {
    //. . .
    Cache cache = emf.getCache();
    boolean inCache = cache.contains(Student.class, 1234);
    //. . .
}
```

A specific entity can be cleared:

```
cache.evict(Student.class, 1234);
```

All entities of a class can be invalidated:

```
cache.evict(Student.class);
```

And the complete cache can be invalidated as:

```
cache.evictAll();
```

A standard set of query hints are also available to allow refreshing or bypassing the cache. The query hints are specified as `javax.persistence.cache.retrieveMode` and `javax.persistence.cache.storeMode` properties on the `Query` object. The first property is used to specify the behavior when data is retrieved by the `find` methods and by queries. The second property is used to specify the behavior when data is read from the database and committed into the database:

```
Query query = em.createQuery("SELECT s FROM Student s");
query.setHint("javax.persistence.cache.storeMode",
              CacheStoreMode.BYPASS);
```

The property values are defined on `CacheRetrieveMode` and `CacheStoreMode` enums and explained in Table 4-2.

Table 4-2. CacheStoreMode and CacheRetrieveMode values

Cache query hint	Description
CacheStore Mode.BYPASS	Don't insert into cache.
CacheStore Mode.REFRESH	Insert/update entity data into cache when read from database and when committed into database.
CacheStoreMode.USE	Insert/update entity data into cache when read from database and when committed into database; this is the default behavior.
CacheRetrieve Mode.BYPASS	Bypass the cache: get data directly from the database.
CacheRetrieve Mode.USE	Read entity data from the cache; this is the default behavior.

CHAPTER 5

Enterprise JavaBeans

Enterprise JavaBeans (EJB) is defined as JSR 318, and the complete specification can be downloaded from *http://jcp.org/aboutJava/communityprocess/mrel/jsr318/index.html*.

Enterprise JavaBeans are used for the development and deployment of component-based distributed applications that are scalable, transactional, and secure. An EJB typically contains the business logic that operates on the enterprise's data. The service information, such as transaction and security attributes, may be specified in the form of metadata annotations, or separately in an XML deployment descriptor.

A bean instance is managed at runtime by a container. The bean is accessed on the client and is mediated by the container in which it is deployed. The client can also be on the server in the form of a managed bean, a CDI bean, or a servlet of some sort. In any case, the EJB container provides all the plumbing required for an enterprise application. This allows the application developer to focus on the business logic and not worry about low-level transaction and state management details, remoting, concurrency, multithreading, connection pooling, or other complex low-level APIs.

There are three types of enterprise beans:

- Session beans
- Message-driven beans
- Entity beans

Entity beans are marked for pruning in the EJB 3.1 version of the specification and thus will not be discussed here. It is recommended to use the Java Persistence API for all the persistence and object/relational mapping functionality.

Stateful Session Beans

A stateful session bean contains conversational state for a specific client. The state is stored in the session bean instance's field values, its associated interceptors and their instance field values, and all the objects and their instances' field values reachable by following Java object references.

A simple stateful session bean can be defined by using @Stateful:

```
package org.sample;

@Stateful
public class Cart {
    List<String> items;

    public ShoppingCart() {
        items = new ArrayList<Item>();
    }

    public void addItem(String item) {
        items.add(item);
    }

    public void removeItem(String item) {
        items.remove(item);
    }

    public void purchase() {
      //. . .
    }
```

```
    @Remove
    public void remove() {
        items = null;
    }
}
```

This is a POJO marked with the `@Stateful` annotation. That's all it takes to convert a POJO to a stateful session bean. All public methods of the bean may be invoked by a client. The method `remove` is marked with the `@Remove` annotation and is called before the bean is removed. This method is called by the container when a bean is removed and is not expected to be called by a client. Removing a stateful session bean means that the instance state specific for that client is gone.

This style of bean declaration is called as a *no-interface* view. Such a bean is only locally accessible to clients packaged in the same archive. If the bean needs to be remotely accessible, it must define a separate business interface annotated with `@Remote`:

```
@Remote
public interface Cart {
    public void addItem(String item);
    public void removeItem(String item);
    public void purchase();
}

@Stateful
public class CartBean implements Cart {
    public float addItem(String item) {
        //. . .
    }

    public void removeItem(String item) {
        //. . .
    }

    //. . .
}
```

Now the bean is injected using the interface:

```
@EJB Cart cart;
```

A client of this stateful session bean can access this bean:

```
@EJB ShoppingCart cart;

cart.addItem("Apple");
cart.addItem("Mango");
cart.addItem("Kiwi");
cart.purchase();
```

The PostConstruct and PreDestroy lifecycle callback methods are available for stateful session beans.

An EJB container may decide to *passivate* a stateful session bean to some form of secondary storage and then *activate* it again. The container takes care of saving and restoring the state of the bean. However, if there are nonserializable objects such as open sockets or JDBC connections, they need to be explicitly closed and restored back as part of that process. The @PrePassivate lifecycle callback method is invoked to clean up resources before the bean is passivated, and the PostActivate callback method is invoked to restore the resources.

Stateless Session Beans

A stateless session bean does not contain any conversational state for a specific client. All instances of a stateless bean are equivalent, so the container can choose to delegate a client-invoked method to any available instance. Since stateless session beans do not contain any state, they don't need to be passivated.

A simple stateless session bean can be defined by using @Stateless:

```
package org.sample;

@Stateless
public class AccountSessionBean {
    public float withdraw() {
        //. . .
    }

    public void deposit(float amount) {
```

```
        //. . .
    }
}
```

This is a POJO marked with the `@Stateless` annotation. That's all it takes to convert a POJO to a stateless session bean. All public methods of the bean may be invoked by a client.

This stateless session bean can be accessed by using `@EJB`:

```
@EJB AcountSessionBean account;
account.withdraw();
```

This style of bean declaration is called as a *no-interface* view. Such a bean is only locally accessible to clients packaged in the same archive. If the bean needs to be remotely accessible, it must define a separate business interface annotated with `@Remote`:

```
@Remote
public interface Account {
    public float withdraw();
    public void deposit(float amount);
}

@Stateless
public class AccountSessionBean implements Account {
    public float withdraw() {
        //. . .
    }

    public void deposit(float amount) {
        //. . .
    }
}
```

Now the bean is injected using the interface:

```
@EJB Account account;
```

The `PostConstruct` and `PreDestroy` lifecycle callbacks are supported for stateless session beans.

The `PostConstruct` callback method is invoked after the no-args constructor is invoked and all the dependencies have been injected, and before the first business method is invoked on the bean. This method is typically where all the resources required for the bean are initialized.

The `PreDestroy` lifecycle callback is called before the instance is removed by the container. This method is where all the resources acquired during `PostConstruct` are released.

As stateless beans do not store any state, the container can pool the instances and all of them are treated equally from a client's perspective. Any instance of the bean can be used to service the client's request.

Singleton Session Beans

A singleton session bean is a session bean component that is instantiated once per application and provides easy access to shared state. If the container is distributed over multiple virtual machines, each application will have one instance of the singleton for each JVM. A singleton session bean is explicitly designed to be shared and supports concurrency.

A simple singleton session bean can be defined by using `@Singleton`:

```
@Singleton
public class MySingleton {
    //. . .
}
```

The container is responsible for when to initialize a singleton bean instance. However, the bean may be optionally marked for eager initialization by annotating with `@Startup`:

```
@Startup
@Singleton
public class MySingleton {
    //. . .
}
```

The container now initializes all such startup-time singletons, executing the code marked in `@PostConstruct`, before the application becomes available and any client request is serviced.

An explicit initialization of singleton session beans may be specified using @DependsOn:

```
@Singleton
public class Foo {
    //. . .
}

@DependsOn("Foo")
@Singleton
public class Bar {
    //. . .
}
```

The container ensures that Foo bean is initialized before Bar bean.

A singleton bean supports PostConstruct and PreDestroy life-cycle callback methods.

A singleton bean always supports concurrent access. By default a singleton bean is marked for container-managed concurrency, but alternatively may be marked for bean-managed concurrency.

Container-managed concurrency is based on method-level locking metadata where each method is associated with either a Read (shared) or Write (exclusive) lock. A Read lock allows concurrent invocations of the method. A Write lock waits for the processing of one invocation to complete before allowing the next invocation to proceed.

By default, a Write lock is associated with each method of the bean. The @Lock(LockType.READ) and @Lock(LockType.WRITE) annotations are used to specify concurrency locking attributes. These annotations may be specified on the class, a business method of the class, or both. A value specified on a method overrides a value specified on the bean.

Bean-managed concurrency requires the developer to manage concurrency using Java language–level synchronization primitives such as synchronized and volatile.

Message-Driven Beans

A message-driven bean (MDB) is a container-managed bean that is used to process messages asynchronously. An MDB can implement any messaging type, but is most commonly used to process Java Message Service (JMS) messages. These beans are stateless and are invoked by the container when a JMS message arrives at the destination. A session bean can receive a JMS message synchronously, but a message-driven bean can receive a message asynchronously.

A POJO can be converted to a message-driven bean by using @MessageDriven:

```java
@MessageDriven(mappedName = "myDestination")
public class MyMessageBean implements MessageListener {

    @Override
    public void onMessage(Message message) {
        try {
            // process the message
        } catch (JMSException ex) {
            //. . .
        }
    }
}
```

In this code, @MessageDriven defines the bean to be a message-driven bean. The mappedName attribute specifies the JNDI name of the JMS destination from which the bean will consume the message. The bean must implement the MessageListener interface that provides only one method, onMessage. This method is called by the container whenever a message is received by the message-driven bean and contains the application-specific business logic.

This code shows how a message received by the onMessage method is a text message and the message body can be retrieved and displayed:

```java
public void onMessage(Message message) {
    try {
        TextMessage tm = (TextMessage)message;
```

```
        System.out.println(tm.getText());
    } catch (JMSException ex) {
        //. . .
    }
}
```

Even though a message-driven bean cannot be invoked directly by a session bean, it can still invoke other session beans. A message-driven bean can also send JMS messages.

`@MessageDriven` can take additional attributes to configure the bean. For example, the `activationConfig` property can take an array of `ActivationConfigProperty` that provides information to the deployer about the configuration of the bean in its operational environment.

Table 5-1 defines the standard set of configuration properties that are supported.

Table 5-1. Message-driven bean ActivationConfig properties

Property name	Description
acknowledgeMode	Specifies JMS acknowledgment mode for the message delivery when bean-managed transaction demarcation is used. Supported values are `Auto_acknowledge` (default) or `Dups_ok_acknowledge`.
messageSelector	Specifies JMS message selector to be used in determining which messages an MDB receives.
destinationType	Specifies whether the MDB is to be used with a Queue or Topic. Supported values are `javax.jms.Queue` or `javax.jms.Topic`.
subscriptionDurability	If MDB is used with a Topic, specifies whether a durable or nondurable subscription is used. Supported values are `Durable` or `NonDurable`.

A single message-driven bean can process messages from multiple clients concurrently. Just like stateless session beans, the container can pool the instances and allocate enough bean instances to handle the number of messages at a given time. All instances of the bean are treated equally.

A message is delivered to a message-driven bean within a transaction context, so all operations within the `onMessage` method are part of a single transaction. The transaction context is propagated to the other methods invoked from within `onMessage`.

`MessageDrivenContext` may be injected in a message-driven bean. This provides access to the runtime message-driven context that is associated with the instance for its lifetime:

```
@Resource
MessageDrivenContext mdc;

public void onMessage(Message message) {
    try {
        TextMessage tm = (TextMessage)message;
        System.out.println(tm.getText());
    } catch (JMSException ex) {
        mdc.setRollbackOnly();
    }
}
```

Portable Global JNDI Names

A session bean can be packaged in an *ejb-jar* file or within a web application module (*.war*). An optional EJB deployment descriptor, *ejb-jar.xml*, providing additional information about the deployment may be packaged in an *ejb-jar* or *.war* file. The *ejb-jar.xml* file can be packaged as either *WEB-INF/ejb-jar.xml* or as *META-INF/ejb-jar.xml* within one of the *WEB-INF/lib* JAR files, but not both.

A local or no-interface bean packaged in the *.war* file is accessible only to other components within the same *.war* file, but a bean marked with `@Remote` is remotely accessible independent of its packaging. The *ejb-jar* file may be deployed by itself or packaged within an *.ear* file. The beans packaged in this *ejb-jar* can be accessed remotely.

This EJB can also be accessed using a portable global JNDI name using the following syntax:

```
java:global[/<app-name>]
          /<module-name>
          /<bean-name>
          [!<fully-qualified-interface-name>]
```

<app-name> applies only if the session bean is packaged with an *.ear* file.

<module-name> is the name of the module in which the session bean is packaged.

<bean-name> is the *ejb-name* of the enterprise bean.

If the bean exposes only one client interface (or alternatively has only a no-interface view), the bean is also exposed with an additional JNDI name using the following syntax:

```
java:global[/<app-name>]/<module-name>/<bean-name>
```

The stateless session bean is also available through the java:app and java:module namespaces.

If the AccountSessionBean is packaged in *bank.war*, then the following JNDI entries are exposed:

```
java:global/bank/AccountSessionBean
java:global/bank/AccountSessionBean
    !org.sample.AccountSessionBean
java:app/AccountSessionBean
java:app/AccountSessionBean!org.sample.AccountSessionBean
java:module/AccountSessionBean
java:module/AccountSessionBean!org.sample
.AccountSessionBean
```

Transactions

A bean may use programmatic transaction in the bean code, and is called a *bean-managed transaction*. Alternatively, a declarative transaction may be used in which the transactions are managed automatically by the container, and is called a *container-managed transaction*. Container-managed transaction is the default. The @TransactionManagement annotation is used to declare whether the session bean or message-driven bean uses a bean-managed or container-managed transaction.

The value of this annotation is either `CONTAINER` (the default) or `BEAN`.

Bean-managed transaction requires you to specify `@TransactionManagement(BEAN)` on the class and use the `javax.transaction.UserTransaction` interface. Within the business method, a transaction is started using `UserTransaction.begin` and committed with `UserTransaction.commit`:

```
@Stateless
@TransactionManagement(BEAN)
public class AccountSessionBean {
    @Resource javax.transaction.UserTransaction tx;

    public float deposit() {
        //. . .
        tx.begin();
        //. . .
        tx.commit();
        //. . .
    }
}
```

Container-managed transaction is the default and does not require you to specify any additional annotations on the class. The EJB container implements all the low-level transaction protocols, such as the two phase commit protocol between a transaction manager and a database system or messaging provider, to honor the transactional semantics. The changes to the underlying resources are all committed or rolled back.

A stateless session bean using a container-managed transaction can use `@TransactionAttribute` to specify transaction attributes on the bean class or the method. Specifying the `TransactionAttribute` on a bean class means that it applies to all applicable methods of the bean. The absence of `TransactionAttribute` on the bean class is equivalent to the specification of `TransactionAttribute(REQUIRED)` on the bean.

A bean class using a container-managed transaction looks like:

```
@Stateless
public class AccountSessionBean {
```

```
    public float deposit() {
        //. . .
    }
}
```

There are no additional annotations specified on the bean class or the method.

The `@TransactionAttribute` values and meaning are defined in Table 5-2.

Table 5-2. @TransactionAttribute values

Value	Description
MANDATORY	Always called in client's transaction context. If the client calls with a transaction context then it behaves as REQUIRED. If the client calls without a transaction context, then the container throws the `javax.ejb.EJBTransactionRequiredException`.
REQUIRED	If the client calls with a transaction context, then it is propagated to the bean. Otherwise container starts a new transaction before delegating a call to the business method and attempts to commit the transaction when the business process has completed.
REQUIRES_NEW	The container always starts a new transaction context before delegating a call to the business method and attempts to commit the transaction when the business process has completed. If the client calls with a transaction context, then the suspended transaction is resumed after the new transaction has committed.
SUPPORTS	If the client calls with a transaction context, then it behaves as REQUIRED. If the client calls without a transaction context, then it behaves as NOT_SUPPORTED.
NOT_SUPPORTED	If the client calls with a transaction context, then the container suspends and resumes the association of transaction context before and after the business method is invoked. If the client calls without a transaction context, then no new transaction context is created.
NEVER	Client is required to call without a transaction context. If the client calls with a transaction context, then the container throws `javax.ejb.EJBException`. If the client calls without a transaction context, then it behaves as NOT_SUPPORTED.

The `container-transaction` element in the deployment descriptor may be used instead of annotations to specify the transaction attributes. The values specified in the deployment descriptor override or supplement the transaction attributes specified in the annotation.

Only the `NOT_SUPPORTED` and `REQUIRED` transaction attributes may be used for message-driven beans. A JMS message is delivered to its final destination after the transaction is committed, so the client will not receive the reply within the same transaction.

Asynchronous

Each method of a session bean is invoked synchronously (i.e., the client is blocked until the server-side processing is complete and the result returned). A session bean may tag a method for asynchronous invocation, and a client can then invoke that method asynchronously.

This allows control to return to the client before the container dispatches the instance to a bean. The asynchronous operations must have a return type of `void` or `Future<V>`. The methods with a `void` return type are used for a *fire and forget* pattern. The other version allows the client to retrieve a result value, check for exceptions, or attempt to cancel any in-progress invocations.

The `@Asynchronous` annotation is used to mark a specific method (method level) or all methods (class level) of the bean as asynchronous. Here is an example of a stateless session bean that is tagged as asynchronous at the class level:

```
@Stateless
@Asynchronous
public class MyAsyncBean {
    public Future<Integer> addNumbers(int n1, int n2) {
        Integer result;
        result = n1 + n2;
        // simulate a long running query
        . . .
```

```
            return new AsyncResult(result);
    }
}
```

The method signature returns `Future<Integer>` and the return type is `AsyncResult(Integer)`. `AsyncResult` is a new class introduced in EJB 3.1 that wraps the result of an asynchronous method as a `Future` object. Behind the scenes, the value is retrieved and sent to the client. Adding any new methods to this class will automatically make them asynchronous as well.

This session bean can be injected and invoked in any Java EE component:

```
@EJB MyAsyncBean asyncBean;

Future<Integer> future = asyncBean.addNumbers(10, 20);
```

The methods on the `Future` API are used to query the availability of a result with `isDone` or cancel the execution with `cancel(boolean mayInterruptIfRunning)`.

The client transaction context does not propagate to the asynchronous business method. This means that the semantics of the `REQUIRED` transaction attribute on an asynchronous method are exactly the same as `REQUIRES_NEW`.

The client security principal propagates to the asynchronous business method. This means the security context propagation behaves the same way for synchronous and asynchronous method execution.

Timers

The EJB Timer Service is a container-managed service that allows callbacks to be scheduled for time-based events. These events are scheduled according to a calendar-based schedule at a specific time, after a specific elapsed duration, or at specific recurring intervals.

There are multiple ways time-based events can be scheduled:

- Automatic timers based upon the metadata specified using @Schedule
- Programmatically using Timer Service
- Methods marked with @Timeout
- Deployment descriptors

The first way to execute time-based methods is by marking any method of the bean with @Schedule:

```
@Stateless
public class MyTimer {

    @Schedule(hour="*", minute="*", second="*/10"),
    public void printTime() {
        //. . .
    }
}
```

In this code, the printTime method is called every 10th second of every minute of every hour. @Schedule also takes year and month fields, with a default value of * indicating to execute this method each month of all years.

The EJB container reads the @Schedule annotations and automatically creates timers.

Table 5-3 shows some samples that can be specified using @Schedule and their meanings.

Table 5-3. @Schedule expressions and meanings

@Schedule	Meaning
hour="1,2,20"	1 am, 2 am, and 10 pm on all days of the year
dayOfWeek="Mon-Fri"	Monday, Tuesday, Wednesday, Thursday, and Friday, at midnight (based upon the default values of hour, minute, and second)
minute="30", hour="4", timezone="America/Los_Angeles"	Every morning at 4:30 US Pacific Time
dayOfMonth="-1,Last"	One day before the last day and the last day of the month at midnight

@Schedules may be used to specify multiple timers.

Note that there is no need for an, @Startup annotation here, as lifecycle callback methods are not required. Each re-deploy of the application will automatically delete and re-create all the schedule-based timers.

Interval timers can be easily created by using ScheduleExpression.start() and end() methods. The single-action timer can be easily created by specifying fixed values for each field:

```
@Schedule(year="A",
          month="B",
          dayOfMonth="C",
          hour="D",
          minute="E",
          second="F")
```

Timers are not for real time, as the container interleaves the calls to a timeout callback method with the calls to the business methods and the lifecycle callback methods of the bean. So the timed-out method may not be invoked at exactly the time specified at timer creation.

The Timer Service allows for programmatic creation and cancellation of timers. Programmatic timers can be created using createXXX methods on TimerService. The method to be invoked at the scheduled time may be the ejbTimeout method from TimedObject:

```
package org.sample;

@Singleton
@Startup
public class MyTimer implements TimedObject {
  @Resource TimerService timerService;

  @PostConstruct
  public void initTimer() {
    if (timerService.getTimers() != null) {
      for (Timer timer : timerService.getTimers()) {
        timer.cancel();
      }
    }
    timerService.createCalendarTimer(
```

```
          new ScheduleExpression().
            hour("*").
            minute("*").
            second("*/10"),
          new TimerConfig("myTimer", true)
    );

    @Override
    public void ejbTimeout(Timer timer) {
        //. . .

    }
}
```

The `initTimer` method is a lifecycle callback method that cleans up any previously created timers and then creates a new timer that triggers every 10th second. The `ejbTimeout` method, implemented from the `TimedObject` interface, is invoked every time the timeout occurs. The `timer` parameter in this method can be used to cancel the timer, can get information on when the next timeout will occur, information about the timer itself, and other relevant data.

Note that the timers are created in the lifecycle callback methods, thus ensuring that they are ready before any business method on the bean is invoked.

The third way to create timers is for a method to have the following signatures:

```
void <METHOD>() {
    //. . .
}
void <METHOD>(Timer timer) {
    //. . .
}
```

The method needs to be marked with `@Timeout`:

```
public class MyTimer {

    //. . .

    @Timeout
    public void timeout(Timer timer) {
        //. . .
```

```
        }
    }
```

The fourth way to create timers is where a method can be tagged for execution on a timer expiration using *ejb-jar.xml*. Let's say the method looks like:

```
public class MyTimer {
    public void timeout(Timer timer) {
        //. . .
    }
}
```

The method `timeout` can be converted into a timer method by adding the following fragment to *ejb-jar.xml*:

```
<enterprise-beans>
    <session>
        <ejb-name>MyTimer</ejb-name>
        <ejb-class>org.sample.MyTimer</ejb-class>
        <session-type>Stateless</session-type>
        <timer>
            <schedule>
                <second>*/10</second>
                <minute>*</minute>
                <hour>*</hour>
                <month>*</month>
                <year>*</year>
            </schedule>
            <timeout-method>
                <method-name>timeout</method-name>
                <method-params>
                    <method-param>
                        javax.ejb.Timer
                    </method-param>
                </method-params>
            </timeout-method>
        </timer>
    </session>
</enterprise-beans>
```

Timers can be created in stateless session beans, singleton session beans, and message-driven beans, but not stateful session beans. This functionality may be added to a future version of the specification.

Timers are persistent by default, and need to made nonpersistent programmatically (`TimerConfig.setPersistent(false)`) or automatically (by adding `persistent=false` on `@Schedule`).

The timer-based events can only be scheduled in stateless session beans and singleton session beans.

Embeddable API

The Embeddable EJB API allows client code and its corresponding enterprise beans to run within the same JVM and class loader. The client uses the bootstrapping API from the `javax.ejb` package to start the container and identify the set of enterprise bean components for execution. This provides better support for testing, offline processing, and executing EJB components within a Java SE environment.

The sample code below shows how to write a test case that starts the embeddable EJB container, looks up the loaded EJB using Portable Global JNDI Name, and invokes a method on it:

```
public void testEJB() throws NamingException {
    EJBContainer ejbC = EJBContainer.createEJBContainer();
    Context ctx = ejbC.getContext();
    MyBean bean = (MyBean) ctx.lookup
        ("java:global/classes/org/sample/MyBean");
    assertNotNull(bean);
    //. . .
    ejbC.close();
}
```

The embeddable EJB container uses the JVM classpath to scan for the EJB modules to be loaded. The client can override this behavior during setup by specifying an alternative set of target modules:

```
Properties props = new Properties();
props.setProperty(EJBContainer.EMBEDDABLE_MODULES_PROPERTY,
                  "bar");
EJBContainer ejbC = EJBContainer.createEJBContainer(props);
```

This code will load only the **bar** EJB module in the embeddable container.

Table 5-4 explains the properties that may be used to configure the EJB container.

Table 5-4. Embeddable EJB container initialization properties

Name	Type	Purpose
`javax.ejb.embeddable.initial` or `EJBContainer.EMBEDDABLE_INITIAL_PROPERTY`	String	Fully qualified name of embeddable container provider class to be used for this application.
`javax.ejb.embeddable.modules` or `EJBContainer.EMBEDDABLE_MODULES_PROPERTY`	String or String[] java.io.File or java.io.File[]	Modules to be initialized. If included in the classpath, specified as `String` or `String[]`. If not in the classpath, specified as `File` or `File[]` where each object is referring to an *ejb-jar* or exploded *ejb-jar* directory.
`javax.ejb.embeddable.appName` or `EJBContainer.EMBEDDABLE_APP_NAME_PROPERTY`	String	Application name for an EJB module. It corresponds to the `<app-name>` portion of the Portable Global JNDI Name syntax.

The embeddable container implementation may support additional properties.

EJB.Lite

The full set of EJB functionality may not be required for all enterprise applications. As explained earlier, the web profile offers a reasonably complete stack composed of standard APIs, and is capable out-of-the-box for addressing a wide variety of web applications. The applications targeted toward web profiles will want to use transactions, security, and other functionality defined in the EJB specification. EJB.Lite was created to meet that need.

EJB.Lite is a minimum set of the complete EJB functionality. No new functionality is defined as part of EJB.Lite; it is merely a proper subset of the full functionality. This allows the EJB API to be used in applications that may have much smaller installation and runtime footprints than a typical full Java EE implementation.

Table 5-5 highlights the difference between EJB 3.1 Lite and EJB 3.1 Full API.

Table 5-5. Difference between EJB 3.1 Lite and EJB 3.1 Full API

	EJB 3.1 Lite	EJB 3.1 Full API
Session beans	✓	✓
Message-Driven beans	✗	✓
2.x/1.x/CMP/BMP Entity beans	✗	✓
Java persistence 2.0	✓	✓
Local / No-interface	✓	✓
3.0 Remote	✗	✓
2.x Remote / Home component	✗	✓
JAX-WS Web service endpoint	✗	✓
JAX-RPC Web service endpoint	✗	✓
EJB Timer service	✗	✓
Asynchronous session bean invocations	✗	✓
Interceptors	✓	✓
RMI-IIOP Interoperability	✗	✓
Container-managed transactions / Bean-managed transactions	✓	✓
Declarative and programmatic security	✓	✓
Embeddable API	✓	✓

Functionality defined by EJB.Lite is available in a Java EE web profile–compliant application server. A full Java EE–compliant application server is required to implement the complete set of functionality.

CHAPTER 6

Contexts and Dependency Injection

Contexts and Dependency Injection (CDI) is defined as JSR 299, and the complete specification can be downloaded from *http://jcp.org/aboutJava/communityprocess/final/jsr299/index.html*.

CDI defines a type-safe dependency injection mechanism in the Java EE platform. A bean specifies only the type and semantics of other beans it depends upon, without a string name and using the type information available in the Java object model. This allows compile-time validation in addition to deployment. It also provides for easy refactoring.

The injection request need not be aware of the actual lifecycle, concrete implementation, threading model, or other clients of the bean. This "strong typing, loose coupling" makes your code easier to maintain. The bean so injected has a well-defined lifecycle and is bound to *lifecycle contexts*. The injected bean is also called a *contextual instance* because it is always injected in a context.

Almost any POJO can be injected as a CDI bean. This includes EJBs, JNDI resources, entity classes, and persistence units and contexts. Even the objects that were earlier created by a factory method can now be easily injected. Specifically, CDI allows

EJB components to be used as JSF managed beans, thus bridging the gap between the transactional and the web tier. It is also integrated with Unified Expression Language (UEL), allowing any contextual object to be used directly within a JSF or JSP page.

Injection Points

A bean may be injected at field, method, or constructor using @Inject.

The following code shows a Greeting interface, a POJO SimpleGreeting as its implementation, and injection of the interface as a field in GreetingService:

```java
public interface Greeting {
    public String greet(String name);
}

public class SimpleGreeting implements Greeting {
    public String greet(String name) {
        return "Hello" + name;
    }
}

@Stateless
public class GreetingService {
    @Inject Greeting greeting;

    public String greet(String name) {
        return greeting.greet(name);
    }
}
```

@Inject specifies the injection point, Greeting specifies what needs to be injected, and greeting is the variable that gets the injection.

A bean may define one or more methods as targets of injection as well:

```
Greeting greeting;

@Inject
public setGreeting(Greeting greeting) {
    this.greeting = greeting;
}
```

Finally, a bean can have at most one constructor marked with @Inject:

```
Greeting greeting;

@Inject
public SimpleGreeting(Greeting greeting) {
    this.greeting = greeting;
}
```

All method parameters are then automatically injected. This constructor may have any number of parameters, and all of them are injection points. A constructor marked with @Inject need not have public access. This allows a bean with constructor injection to be immutable.

Here is the bean initialization sequence:

1. Default constructor or the one annotated with @Inject.
2. All fields of the bean annotated with @Inject.
3. All methods of the bean annotated with @Inject (the call order is not portable, though).
4. @PostConstruct method, if any.

Qualifier and Alternative

Qualifier allows you to uniquely specify a bean to be injected among its multiple implementations. For example, this code declares a new qualifier, @Fancy:

```
@Qualifier
@Retention(RUNTIME)
@Target({METHOD, FIELD, PARAMETER, TYPE})
public @interface Fancy {
}
```

This defines a new implementation of the `Greeting` interface:

```
@Fancy
public class FancyGreeting implements Greeting {
    public String greet(String name) {
        return "Nice to meet you, hello" + name;
    }
}
```

and injects it in the `GreetingService` by specifying `@Fancy` as the qualifer:

```
@Stateless
public class GreetingService {
    @Inject @Fancy Greeting greeting;

    public String sayHello(String name) {
        return greeting.greet(name);
    }
}
```

This removes any direct dependency to any particular implementation of the interface. Qualifiers may take parameters for further discrimination. Multiple qualifiers may be specified at an injection point.

Table 6-1 lists the built-in qualifiers and their meanings.

Table 6-1. Built-in CDI qualifiers

Qualifier	Description
@Named	String-based qualifier, required for usage in Expression Language
@Default	Default qualifier on all beans without an explicit qualifier, except @Named
@Any	Default qualifier on all beans except @New
@New	Allows the application to obtain a new instance independent of the declared scope

Using the `SimpleGreeting` and `FancyGreeting` implementations defined earlier, the injection points are explained below:

```
@Inject Greeting greeting;
@Inject @Default Greeting greeting;
@Inject @Any @Default Greeting greeting;
```

The three injection points are equivalent, as each bean has `@Default` and `@Any` (except for `@New`) qualifiers and specifying them does not provide any additional information. The `Simple Greeting` bean is injected in each statement. Thus:

```
@Inject @Any @Fancy Greeting greeting;
```

will inject `FancyGreeting` implementation. This is because specifying `@Fancy` on `FancyGreeting` means it does not have the `@Default` qualifier. This statement:

```
@Inject @Any Greeting greeting;
```

will result in *ambiguous dependency* and require further qualification of the bean by specifying `@Default` or `@Fancy`.

The use of `@Named` as an injection point qualifier is not recommended, except in the case of integration with legacy code that uses string-based names to identify beans.

The beans marked with `@Alternative` are unavailable for injection, lookup, or EL resolution. They need to be explicitly enabled in *beans.xml* using `<alternatives>`:

```
@Alternative
public class SimpleGreeting implements Greeting {
    //. . .
}

@Fancy @Alternative
public class FancyGreeting implements Greeting {
    //. . .
}
```

Now the following injection will give an error about *unresolved dependency*:

```
@Inject Greeting greeting;
```

because both the beans are disabled for injection. This error can be resolved by explicitly enabling one of the beans in *beans.xml*:

```
<beans
    xmlns="http://java.sun.com/xml/ns/javaee"
    xmlns:xsi="http://www.w3.org/2001/XMLSchema-instance"
    xsi:schemaLocation="
```

```
        http://java.sun.com/xml/ns/javaee
        http://java.sun.com/xml/ns/javaee/beans_1_0.xsd">
    <alternatives>
        <class>org.sample.FancyGreeting</class>
    </alternatives>
</beans>
```

@Alternative allows multiple implementations of a bean with the same qualifiers to be packaged in the *.war* file and selectively enabled by changing the deployment descriptor based upon the environment. For example, this can allow you to target separate beans for injection in development, testing, and production environments by enabling the classes in *beans.xml*. This provides deployment-type polymorphism.

Producer and Disposer

@Inject and @Qualifier provide static injection of a bean (i.e., the concrete type of the bean to be injected is known). However, this may not always be possible. The *producer methods* provide runtime polymorphism where the concrete type of the bean to be injected may vary at runtime, the injected object may not even be a bean, and objects may require custom initialization. This is similar to the well known *factory pattern*.

Here is an example that shows how List<String> can be made available as a target for injection:

```
@Produces
public List<String> getGreetings() {
    List<String> response = new ArrayList<String>();
    //. . .
    return response;
}
```

In this code, the getGreetings method can populate List<String> from a DataSource or by invoking some other external operation.

And now it can be injected as:

```
@Inject List<String> list;
```

By default, a bean is injected in @Dependent scope, but it can be changed by explicitly specifying the required scope. Let's say Connection is a bean that encapsulates a connection to a resource, for example a database accessible using JDBC, and User provides credentials to the resource. The following code shows how a Connection bean is available for injection in request scope:

```
@Produces @RequestScoped
Connection connect(User user) {
    return createConnection(user.getId(),
user.getPassword());
}
```

Here is another example of how PersistenceContext may be exposed as a type-safe bean. This is the typical code of how an EntityManager is injected:

```
@PersistenceContext(unitName="...")
EntityManager em;
```

All such references can be unified in a single file as:

```
@Produces
@PersistenceContext(unitName="...")
@CustomerDatabase
EntityManager em;
```

where CustomerDatabase is a qualifier. The EntityManager can now be injected as:

```
@Inject @CustomerDatabase
EntityManager em;
```

Similarly, JMS factories and destinations can be injected in a type-safe way.

Some objects that are made available for injection using @Produces may require explicit destruction. For example, the JMS factories and destinations need to be closed. Here is a code example that shows how the Connection produced earlier may be closed:

```
void close(@Disposes Connection connection) {
    connection.close();
}
```

Interceptors and Decorators

Interceptors are used to implement cross-cutting concerns, such as logging, auditing, and security, from the business logic.

The specification is not entirely new, as the concept already existed in the EJB 3.0 specification. However, it is now abstracted at a higher level so that it can be more generically applied to a broader set of specifications in the platform. Interceptors do what they say—they intercept on invocations and lifecycle events on an associated target class. Basically, an interceptor is a class whose methods are invoked when business methods on a target class are invoked, lifecycle events such as methods that create/destroy the bean occur, or an EJB timeout method occurs. The CDI specification defines a type-safe mechanism for associating interceptors to beans using interceptor bindings.

An *interceptor binding type* needs to be defined in order to intercept a business method. This can be done by specifying the `@InterceptorBinding` meta-annotation:

```
@InterceptorBinding
@Retention(RUNTIME)
@Target({METHOD,TYPE})
public @interface Logging {
}
```

`@Target` defines the program element to which this interceptor can be applied. In this case, the annotation `@Logging` can be applied to a method or a type (class, interface, or enum).

The interceptor is implemented:

```
@Interceptor
@Logging
public class LoggingInterceptor {
  @AroundInvoke
  public Object log(InvocationContext context)
    throws Exception {
    Logger.getLogger(getClass().getName().
        info(context.getMethod().getName());
    Logger.getLogger(getClass().getName().
        info(context.getParameters());
```

```
      return context.proceed();
  }
}
```

Adding the @Interceptor annotation marks this class as an interceptor, and @Logging specifies that this is an implementation of the earlier defined interceptor binding type. @AroundInvoke indicates that this interceptor method interposes on business methods. Only one method of an interceptor may be marked with this annotation. InvocationContext provides context information about the intercepted invocation and operations and can be used to control the behavior of the invocation chain.

This method is printing the name of the business method being invoked and the parameters passed to it.

This interceptor may be attached to any managed bean:

```
@Logging
public class SimpleGreeting {
  //. . .
}
```

Alternatively, individual methods may be logged by attaching the interceptor:

```
public class SimpleGreeting {
  @Logging
  public String greet(String name) {
    //. . .
  }
}
```

Multiple interceptors may be defined using the same interceptor binding.

By default, all interceptors are disabled and need to be explicitly enabled by specifying them in *beans.xml*:

```
<beans xmlns="http://java.sun.com/xml/ns/javaee"
    xmlns:xsi="http://www.w3.org/2001/XMLSchema-instance"
    xsi:schemaLocation="http://java.sun.com/xml/ns/javaee .
    http://java.sun.com/xml/ns/javaee/beans_1_0.xsd">
    <interceptors>
        <class>org.sample.LoggingInterceptor</class>
    </interceptors>
</beans>
```

Note that the actual interceptor implementation class is mentioned here.

Defining interceptor bindings provides one level of indirection, but removes the dependency from the actual interceptor implementation class. It also allows you to vary the actual interceptor implementation based upon the deployment environment as well, and to provide a central ordering of interceptors for that archive. The interceptors are invoked in the order in which they are specified inside the `<interceptors>` element.

Interceptors also support dependency injection. An interceptor that adds basic transactional behavior to a managed bean may be defined:

```
@Interceptor
@Transactional
public class TransactionInterceptor {
  @Resource UserTransaction tx;

  @AroundInvoke
  public Object manageTransaction(
                  InvocationContext context) {
    tx.begin()
    Object response = context.proceed();
    tx.commit();
    return response;
  }
}
```

`UserTransaction` is injected in the interceptor and is then used to start and commit the transaction in the interceptor method. `@Transactional` is a standard interceptor binding type and can be specified on any managed bean or a method thereof to indicate the transactional behavior.

A lifecycle callback interceptor can be implemented:

```
public class LifecycleInterceptor {
    @PostConstruct
    public void init(InvocationContext context) {
        //. . .
    }
}
```

An EJB timeout interceptor can be implemented:

```java
public class TimeoutInterceptor {
    @AroundTimeout
    public Object timeout(InvocationContext context) {
        //. . .
    }
}
```

Decorators are used to implement business concerns. Interceptors are unaware of the business semantics of the invoked bean and thus are more widely applicable; decorators complement interceptors as they are semantic-aware of the business method and applicable to beans of a particular type. A decorator is a bean that implements the bean it decorates and is annotated with @Decorator stereotype:

```java
@Decorator
class MyDecorator implements Greeting {
    public String greet(String name) {
        //. . .
    }
}
```

The decorator class may be abstract, as it may not be implementing all methods of the bean.

A decorator class has a *delegate injection point* that is an injection point for the same type as the beans they decorate. The delegate injection point follows the normal rules for injection and therefore must be an injected field, initializer method parameter, or bean constructor method parameter. This delegate injection point specifies that the decorator is bound to all beans that implement Greeting:

```java
@Inject @Delegate @Any Greeting greeting;
```

A delegate injection point may specify qualifiers, and the decorator is then bound to beans with the same qualifiers.

By default, all decorators are disabled and need to be explicitly enabled by specifying them in *beans.xml*:

```xml
<beans xmlns="http://java.sun.com/xml/ns/javaee"
    xmlns:xsi="http://www.w3.org/2001/XMLSchema-instance"
    xsi:schemaLocation="http://java.sun.com/xml/ns/javaee
```

```
         http://java.sun.com/xml/ns/javaee/beans_1_0.xsd">
    <decorators>
        <class>org.sample.MyDecorator</class>
    </decorators>
</beans>
```

Just like interceptors, this allows you to specify a central ordering of decorators for that archive and vary the set of decorators based upon the deployment environment.

In order of execution, the interceptors for a method are called before the decorators that apply to the method.

Scopes and Contexts

A bean is said to be in a *scope* and is associated with a *context*. The associated context manages the lifecycle and visibility of all beans in that scope. A bean is created once per scope and then reused. When a bean is requested in a particular scope, a new instance is created if it does not exist already. If it does exist, that instance is returned instead. The runtime makes sure the bean in the right scope is created, if required; the client does not have to be scope-aware. This provides loose coupling between the client and the bean to be injected.

There are four predefined scopes and one default scope, as shown in Table 6-2.

Table 6-2. Predefined scopes in CDI

Scope	Description
@RequestScoped	A bean is scoped to a request. The bean is available during a single request and destroyed when the request is complete.
@SessionScoped	A bean is scoped to a session. The bean is shared between all requests that occur in the same HTTP session, holds state throughout the session, and is destroyed when the HTTP session times out or is invalidated.
@ApplicationScoped	A bean is scoped to an application. The bean is created when the application is started, holds state throughout

Scope	Description
	the application, and is destroyed when the application is shut down.
@Conversa tionScoped	A bean is scoped to a conversation and is of two types: *transient* or *long-running*. By default, a bean in this scope is transient, is created with a JSF request, and is destroyed at the end of the request. A transient conversation can be converted to a long-running one using `Conversa tion.begin`. This long-running conversation can be ended using `Conversation.end`. All long-running conversations are scoped to a particular HTTP servlet session and may be propagated to other JSF requests. Multiple parallel conversations can run within a session, each uniquely identified by a string-valued identifier that is either set by the application or generated by the container. This allows multiple tabs in a browser to hold state corresponding to a conversation, unike session cookies that are shared across tabs.
@Dependent	A bean belongs to the dependent pseudoscope. This is the default scope of the bean that does not explicitly declare a scope.

A contextual reference to the bean is not a direct reference to the bean (unless it is in @Dependent scope). Instead, it is a *client proxy object*. This client proxy is responsible for ensuring that the bean instance that receives a method invocation is the instance that is associated with the current context. This allows you to invoke the bean in the current context instead of using a stale reference.

If the bean is in @Dependent scope, then the client holds a direct reference to its instance. A new instance of the bean is bound to the lifecycle of the newly created object. A bean in @Depen dent scope is never shared between multiple injection points. If an @Dependent-scoped bean is used in an EL expression, then an instance of the bean is created for each EL expression. So a wider lifecycle context, such as @RequestScoped or @SessionScoped, needs to be used if the values evaluated by the EL expression need to be accessible in other beans.

A new scope can be defined using the extensible context model (@Contextual, @CreationalContext, @Context interfaces), but that is generally not required by an application developer.

Stereotypes

A stereotype encapsulates *architectural patterns* or *common metadata* for beans that produce recurring roles in a central place. It encapsulates scope, interceptor bindings, qualifiers, and other properties of the role.

A stereotype is a meta-annotation annotated with @Stereotype:

```
@Stereotype
@Retention(RUNTIME)
@Target(TYPE)
//. . .
public @interface MyStereotype { }
```

A stereotype that adds transactional behavior can be defined as:

```
@Stereotype
@Retention(RUNTIME)
@Target(TYPE)
@Transactional
public @interface MyStereotype { }
```

In this code, an interceptor binding defined earlier, @Transactional, is used to define the stereotype. A single interceptor binding defines this stereotype instead of the interceptor binding. However, it allows you to update the stereotype definition later with other scopes, qualifiers, and properties, and those values are then automatically applied on the bean.

It can be specified on a target bean like any other annotation:

```
@MyStereotype
public class MyBean {
    //. . .
}
```

The metadata defined by the stereotype are now applicable on the bean.

A stereotype may declare the default scope of a bean:

```
@Stereotype
@RequestScoped
@Retention(RUNTIME)
@Target(TYPE)
public @interface MyStereotype { }
```

Specifying this stereotype on a bean marks it to have `@RequestScoped` unless the bean explicitly specifies the scope. A stereotype may declare at most one scope.

A stereotype may declare zero, one, or multiple interceptor bindings:

```
@Stereotype
@Transactional
@Logging
@Retention(RUNTIME)
@Target(TYPE)
public @interface MyStereotype { }
```

Adding `@Alternative` to the stereotype definition marks all the target beans to be alternatives.

Stereotypes can be *stacked* together to create new stereotypes as well.

`@Interceptor`, `@Decorator`, and `@Model` are predefined stereotypes. The `@Model` stereotype is predefined:

```
@Named
@RequestScoped
@Stereotype
@Target({TYPE, METHOD})
@Retention(RUNTIME)
public @interface Model {}
```

This stereotype provides a default name for the bean and marks it `@RequestScoped`. Adding this stereotype on a bean will enable it to pass values from a JSF view to a controller, say an EJB.

Events

Events provide an annotation-based event model based upon the *observer* pattern. Event *producers* raise events that are consumed by *observers*. The event object, typically a POJO, carries state from producer to consumer. The producer and the observer are completely decoupled from each other and only communicate using the state.

A producer bean will fire an event using the Event interface:

```
@Inject @Any Event<Customer> event;
//. . .
event.fire(customer);
```

An observer bean with the following method signature will receive the event:

```
void onCustomer(@Observes Customer event) {
    //. . .
}
```

In this code, Customer is carrying the state of the event.

The producer bean can specify a set of qualifiers when injecting the event:

```
@Inject @Any @Added Event<Customer> event;
```

The observer bean's method signature has to match with the exact set of qualifiers in order to receive the events fired by this bean:

```
void onCustomer(@Observes @Added Customer event) {
    //. . .
}
```

Qualifiers with parameters and multiple qualifiers may be specified to further narrow the scope of an observer bean.

By default, an existing instance of the bean or a new instance of the bean is created in the current context to deliver the event. This behavior can be altered so that the event is delivered only if the bean already exists in the current scope:

```
void onCustomer(
        @Observes(
```

```
                notifyObserver= Reception.IF_EXISTS)
            @Added Customer event){
        //. . .
    }
```

Transactional observer methods receive their event notifications during the before or after completion phase of the transaction in which the event was fired. `TransactionPhase` identifies the kind of transactional observer methods, as defined in Table 6-3.

Table 6-3. Transactional observers

Transactional observers	Description
IN_PROGRESS	Default behavior, observers are called immediately
BEFORE_COMPLETION	Observers are called during the before completion phase of the transaction
AFTER_COMPLETION	Observers are called during the after completion phase of the transaction
AFTER_FAILURE	Observers are called during the after completion phase of the transaction, only when the transaction fails
AFTER_SUCCESS	Observers are called during the after completion phase of the transaction, only when the transaction succeeds

For example, the following observer method will be called after the transaction has successfully completed:

```
void onCustomer(
        @Observes(
    during= TransactionPhase.AFTER_SUCCESS)
    @Added Customer event) {
     //. . .
}
```

Portable Extensions

CDI exposes an Service Provider Interface (SPI) allowing portable extensions to extend the functionality of the container easily. A portable extension may integrate with the container by:

- Providing its own beans, interceptors, and decorators to the container

- Injecting dependencies into its own objects using the dependency injection service

- Providing a contextual implementation for a custom scope

- Augmenting or overriding the annotation-based metadata with metadata from some other source

Here is a simple extension:

```java
public class MyExtension implements Extension {

    <T> void processAnnotatedType(
                @Observes ProcessAnnotatedType<T> pat) {
        Logger.global.log(Level.INFO,
            "processing annotation: {0}",
            pat.
                getAnnotatedType().
                getJavaClass().
                getName());
    }
}
```

This extension prints the list of annotations on a bean packaged in a web application.

The extension needs to implement the Extension marker interface. This extension then needs to be registered using the *service provider* mechanism by creating a file named *META-INF/services/javax.enterprise.inject.spi.Extension*. This file contains the fully qualified name of the class implementing the extension:

```
org.sample.MyExtension
```

The bean can listen to a variety of container lifecycle events, as listed in Table 6-4.

Table 6-4. CDI container lifecycle events

Event	When fired ?
BeforeBeanDiscovery	Before the bean discovery process begins
AfterBeanDiscovery	After the bean discovery process is complete
AfterDeployment Validation	After no deployment problems are found and before contexts are created and requests processed
BeforeShutdown	After all requests are finished processing and all contexts destroyed
ProcessAnnotated Type	For each Java class or interface discovered in the application, before the annotations are read
ProcessInjection Target	For every Java EE component class supporting injection
ProcessProducer	For each producer method or field of each enabled bean

Each of these events allows a portable extension to integrate with the container initialization. For example, `Before BeanDiscovery` can be used to add new interceptors, qualifiers, scope, and stereotypes on an existing bean.

`BeanManager` provides operations for obtaining contextual references for beans, along with many other operations of use to portable extensions. It can be injected into the observer methods:

```
<T> void processAnnotatedType(
        @Observes ProcessAnnotatedType<T> pat,
        BeanManager bm) {
    //. . .
}
```

`BeanManager` is also available for field injection and can be looked up using the name `java:comp/BeanManager`.

CHAPTER 7

JavaServer Faces

JavaServer Faces (JSF) is defined as JSR 314, and the complete specification can be downloaded from *http://jcp.org/aboutJava/ communityprocess/final/jsr314/index.html*.

JavaServer Faces is a server-side user interface (UI) framework for Java-based web applications. JSF allows you to:

- Create a web page with a set of reusable UI components following the Model-View-Controller (MVC) design pattern.

- Bind components to a server-side model. This allows a two-way migration of application data with the UI.

- Handle page navigation in response to UI events and model interactions.

- Manage UI component state across server requests.

- Provide a simple model for wiring client-generated events to server-side application code.

- Easily build and reuse custom UI components.

A JSF application consists of:

- A set of web pages in which the UI components are laid out.

- A set of managed beans. One set of beans binds compo-nents to a server-side model (typically CDI beans or

Managed Beans) and another set acts as Controller (typically EJB or CDI beans).

- An optional deployment descriptor, *web.xml*.
- An optional configuration file, *faces-config.xml*.
- An optional set of custom objects such as converters and listeners, created by the application developer.

Facelets

Facelets is the *view declaration language* (aka view handler) for JSF. It is the replacement for JSP, which is now retained only for backward compatibility. New features introduced in version 2 of the JSF specification, such as composite components and Ajax, are only exposed to page authors using facelets. Key benefits of facelets include a powerful templating system, reuse and ease-of-development, better error reporting (including line numbers), and designer-friendliness.

Facelets pages are authored using XHTML 1.0 and Cascading Style Sheets (CSS). An XHTML 1.0 document is a reformulation of an HTML 4 document following the rules of XML 1.0. The pages must conform with the XHTML 1.0 Transitional DTD as described at *http://www.w3.org/TR/xhtml1/#a_dtd _XHTML-1.0-Transitional*.

A simple Facelets page can be defined using XHTML:

```
<?xml version='1.0' encoding='UTF-8' ?>
<!DOCTYPE html
    PUBLIC "-//W3C//DTD XHTML 1.0 Transitional//EN"
 "http://www.w3.org/TR/xhtml1/DTD/xhtml1-transitional.dtd">
<html xmlns="http://www.w3.org/1999/xhtml"
      xmlns:h="http://java.sun.com/jsf/html">
    <h:head>
        <title>My Facelet Page Title</title>
    </h:head>
    <h:body>
        Hello from Facelets
    </h:body>
</html>
```

In this code, an XML prologue is followed by a document type declaration (DTD). The root element of the page is html in the namespace *http://www.w3.org/1999/xhtml*. An XML namespace is declared for the tag library used in the web page. Facelets HTML tags (those beginning with h:) and regular HTML tags are used to add components.

Table 7-1 shows the standard set of tag libraries supported by Facelets.

Table 7-1. Standard tag libraries supported by Facelets

Prefix	URI	Examples
h	*http://java.sun.com/jsf/html*	h:head, h:inputText
f	*http://java.sun.com/jsf/core*	f:facet, f:actionListener
c	*http://java.sun.com/jsp/jstl/core*	c:forEach, c:if
fn	*http://java.sun.com/jsp/jstl/func tions*	fn:toUpperCase, fn:contains
ui	*http://java.sun.com/jsf/facelets*	ui:component, ui:insert

By convention, web pages built with XHTML have a *.xhtml* extension.

Facelets provides Expression Language (EL) integration. This allows two-way data binding between the backing beans and the UI:

```
Hello from Facelets, my name is #{name.value}!
```

In this code, #{name} is an EL that refers to the value field of a request-scoped CDI bean:

```
@Named
@RequestScoped
public class Name {
    private String value;

    //. . .
}
```

It's important to add @Named on a CDI bean to enable its injection in an EL. It is highly recommended to use CDI-compatible beans instead of beans annotated with @javax.faces .bean.ManagedBean.

Similarly, an EJB can be injected in an EL expression:

```
@Stateless
@Named
public class CustomerSessionBean {
    public List<Name> getCustomerNames() {
        //. . .
    }
}
```

This is a stateless session bean and has a business method that returns a list of customer names. @Named marks it for injection in an EL. It can be used in Facelets EL:

```
<h:dataTable value="#{customerSessionBean.customerNames}"
    var="c">
    <h:column>#{c.value}</h:column>
</h:dataTable>
```

In this code, the list of customer names returned is displayed in a table. Notice how the getCustomerNames method is available as a property in the EL.

Facelets also provides compile-time EL validation.

In addition, Facelets provides a powerful templating system that allows you to provide a consistent look-and-feel across multiple pages in a web application. A base page, called a *template*, is created using Facelets templating tags. This page defines a default structure of the page, including placeholders for the content that will be defined in the pages using the template. A *template client page* uses the template and provides actual content for the placeholders defined in the template.

Table 7-2 lists some of the common tags used in template and template client pages.

Table 7-2. Common Facelets tags for a template

Tag	Description
ui:composition	Defines a page layout that optionally uses a template. If the template attribute is used, the children of this tag define the template layout. If not, it's just a group of elements as a composition that can be inserted anywhere. Content outside of this tag is ignored.
ui:insert	Used in a template page and defines the placeholder for inserting content into a template. A matching ui:define tag in the template client page replaces the content.
ui:define	Used in a template client page; defines content that replaces the content defined in a template with a matching ui:insert tag.
ui:component	Inserts a new UI component into the JSF component tree. Any component or content fragment outside this tag is ignored.
ui:fragment	Similar to ui:component, but does not disregard content outside this tag.
ui:include	Includes the document pointed to by the "src" attribute as part of the current Facelets page.

A template page looks like:

```
<h:body>

    <div id="top">
        <ui:insert name="top">
            <h1>Facelets are Cool!</h1>
        </ui:insert>
    </div>

    <div id="content" class="center_content">
        <ui:insert name="content">Content</ui:insert>
    </div>

    <div id="bottom">
        <ui:insert name="bottom">
            <center>Powered by GlassFish</center>
        </ui:insert>
    </div>

</h:body>
```

In this code, the page defines the structure using `<div>` and CSS (not shown here). `ui:insert` defines the content that gets replaced by a template client page.

A template client page looks like:

```
<html xmlns="http://www.w3.org/1999/xhtml"
      xmlns:ui="http://java.sun.com/jsf/facelets"
      xmlns:h="http://java.sun.com/jsf/html">

    <body>

        <ui:composition template="./template.xhtml">

            <ui:define name="content">
                <h:dataTable
         value="#{customerSessionBean.customerNames}"
         var="c">
               <h:column>#{c.value}</h:column>
                </h:dataTable>
            </ui:define>

        </ui:composition>

    </body>
</html>
```

In this code, `ui:insert` with `top` and `bottom` names are not defined, and so those sections are used from the template page. There is a `ui:define` element with a name matching the `ui:insert` element in the template, and so the contents are replaced.

Resource Handling

JSF defines a standard way of handling resources, such as images, CSS, or JavaScript files. These resources are required by a component to be rendered properly.

Such resources can be packaged in */resources* in the web application or in */META-INF/resources* in the classpath. The resources may also be localized, versioned, and collected into libraries.

A resource can be referenced in EL:

```
<a href="#{resource['header.jpg']}">click here</a>
```

In this code, *header.jpg* is bundled in the standard resources directory.

If a resource is bundled in a library *corp* (a folder at the location where resources are packaged), then it can be accessed using the `library` attribute:

```
<h:graphicImage library="corp" name="header.jpg" />
```

JavaScript may be included:

```
<h:outputScript
    name="myScript.js"
    library="scripts"
    target="head"/>
```

In this code, *myScript.js* is a JavaScript resource packaged in the *scripts* directory in the standard resources directory.

A CSS stylesheet can be included:

```
<h:outputStylesheet name="myCSS.css" library="css" />
```

The `ResourceHandler` API provides a programmatic way to serve these resources as well.

Composite Components

Using features of Facelets and Resource Handling, JSF defines a *composite component* as a component that consists of one or more JSF components defined in a Facelets markup file. This *.xhtml* file resides inside of a resource library. This allows you to create a reusable component from an arbitrary region of a page.

The composite component is defined in the *defining page* and used in the *using page*. The defining page defines the metadata (or parameters) using `<cc:interface>` and the implementation using `<cc:implementation>`, where `cc` is the prefix for the *http://java.sun.com/jsf/composite/* namespace. Future versions of the JSF specification may relax the requirement to specify metadata, as it can be derived from the implementation itself.

A composite component can be defined using JSF 1.2 as well, but it requires a much deeper understanding of the JSF lifecycle and also authoring multiple files. JSF2 really simplifies the authoring of composite components using just an XHTML file.

Let's say a Facelet has the following code fragment to display a login form:

```
<h:form>
    <h:panelGrid columns="3">
        <h:outputText value="Name:" />
        <h:inputText value="#{user.name}" id="name"/>
        <h:message for="name" style="color: red" />
        <h:outputText value="Password:" />
        <h:inputText value="#{user.password}"
                     id="password"/>
        <h:message for="password" style="color: red" />
    </h:panelGrid>

    <h:commandButton actionListener=
                        "#{userService.register}"
                     id="loginButton"
                     action="status"
                     value="submit"/>
</h:form>
```

This code renders a table with two rows and three columns, as shown in Figure 7-1.

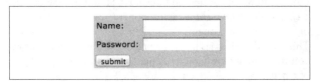

Figure 7-1. JSF Facelets page output in a browser

The first column displays a prompt for the field to be entered; the second column displays an input text box where the data can be entered; and the third column (which shows empty to begin with) is for displaying a message for the corresponding field. The first row binds the input value to the `User.name` field, and the second row binds the input value to the `User.password` field. There is also a command button, and clicking the button invokes the `register` method of the `User Service` bean.

If this login form is to be displayed in multiple pages, then instead of repeating this code everywhere it is beneficial to convert this fragment into a composite component. This requires the code fragment to be copied to an *.xhtml* file, and the file itself is copied in a library in the standard resources directory. Via convention-over-configuration, the fragment is then automatically assigned a namespace and a tag name.

If the fragment shown earlier is copied to *login.xhtml* in the *resources/mycomp* directory, the defining page looks like:

```
<?xml version='1.0' encoding='UTF-8' ?>
<!DOCTYPE html
    PUBLIC "-//W3C//DTD XHTML 1.0 Transitional//EN"
 "http://www.w3.org/TR/xhtml1/DTD/xhtml1-transitional.dtd">
<html xmlns="http://www.w3.org/1999/xhtml"
      xmlns:cc="http://java.sun.com/jsf/composite"
      xmlns:h="http://java.sun.com/jsf/html">

<!-- INTERFACE -->
<cc:interface>
</cc:interface>

<!-- IMPLEMENTATION -->
<cc:implementation>
  <h:form>
    <h:panelGrid columns="3">
      <h:outputText value="Name:" />
      <h:inputText value="#{user.name}" id="name"/>

      <!-- . . . -->

  </h:form>
</cc:implementation>
</html>
```

In this code, `cc:interface` defines metadata that describes the characteristics of the component, such as supported attributes, facets, and attach points for event listeners. `cc:implementation` contains the markup substituted for the composite component.

The namespace of the composite component is constructed by concatenating *http://java.sun.com/jsf/composite/* and *mycomp*. The tag name is the filename without the *.xhtml* suffix in the using page:

```
<html xmlns="http://www.w3.org/1999/xhtml"
      xmlns:mc="http://java.sun.com/jsf/composite/mycomp"

    <!-- . . . -->
    <mc:login/>

</html>
```

Let's say that the code fragment needs to pass different value expressions (instead of `#{user.name}`) and invoke a different method (instead of `#{userService.register}`) when the submit button is clicked in a different using page. The defining page can then pass the values:

```
<!-- INTERFACE -->
<cc:interface>
  <cc:attribute name="name"/>
  <cc:attribute name="password"/>
  <cc:attribute name="actionListener"
      method-signature=
          "void action(javax.faces.event.Event)"
      targets="ccForm:loginButton"/>
</cc:interface>

<!-- IMPLEMENTATION -->
<cc:implementation>
  <h:form id="ccForm">
  <h:panelGrid columns="3">
    <h:outputText value="Name:" />
    <h:inputText value="#{cc.attrs.name}" id="name"/>
    <h:message for="name" style="color: red" />
    <h:outputText value="Password:" />
    <h:inputText value="#{cc.attrs.password}"
        id="password"/>
```

```
    <h:message for="password" style="color: red" />
  </h:panelGrid>

  <h:commandButton id="loginButton"
                   action="status"
                   value="submit"/>
  </h:form>
</cc:implementation>
```

In this code, all the parameters are explicitly specified in
cc:interface for clarity. The third parameter has a targets attribute referring to ccForm:loginButton.

In cc:implementation:

- The h:form has an id attribute. This is required so that the
  button within the form can be explicitly referenced.

- h:inputText is now using #{cc.attrs.xxx} instead of
  #{user.xxx}. #{cc.attrs} is a default EL expression that is
  available for composite component authors and provides
  access to attributes of the current composite component.
  In this case #{cc.attrs} has name and password defined as
  attributes.

- actionListener is an attach point for event listener. It is
  defined as a method-signature and describes the signature
  of the method.

- h:commandButton has an id attribute so that it can be clearly
  identified within the h:form.

The user, password, and actionListener are then passed as required attributes in the using page:

```
<ez:login
    name="#{user.name}"
    password="#{user.password}"
    actionListener="#{userService.register}"/>
```

Now the using page can pass different backing beans, and different business methods can be invoked when the submit button is clicked.

Overall, the composite component provides the following
benefits:

- Follows the Don't Repeat Yourself (DRY) design pattern and allows you to keep code that can be repeated at multiple places in a single file.
- Allows developers to author new components without any Java code or XML configuration.

Ajax

JSF provides native support for adding Ajax capabilities to web pages. It allows *partial view processing*, where only some components from the view are used for processing the response. It also enables *partial page rendering*, where selective components from the page, as opposed to the complete page, are rendered.

There are two ways this support can be enabled:

- Programmatically using JavaScript resources
- Declaratively using f:ajax

Programmatic Ajax integration is enabled using the resource handling mechanism. *jsf.js* is a predefined resource in the **javax.faces** library. This resource contains the JavaScript API that facilitates Ajax interaction with JSF pages. It can be made available in pages using the **outputscript** tag:

```
<h:body>
<!-- . . . -->
<h:outputScript
    name="jsf.js"
    library="javax.faces"
    target="body"/>
<!-- . . . -->
</h:body>
```

An asynchronous request to the server can be made:

```
<h:form prependId="false">
  <h:inputText value="#{user.name}" id="name"/>
  <h:inputText value="#{user.password}" id="password"/>
  <h:commandButton value="Login"
                   type="button"
                   actionListener="#{user.login}"
```

```
      onclick="jsf.ajax.request(this, event, {execute:
'name password', render: 'status'}); return false;"/>

  <h:outputText value="#{user.status}" id="status"/>
</h:form>
```

In this code:

- Two input text fields accept username and password, and the third output field displays the status (whether the user is logged in or not).

- The form has prependId set to false to ensure that the id of each element is preserved as mentioned in the form. Otherwise, JSF prepends the form's id to the id of its children.

- The command button has an actionListener identifying the method in the backing bean to be invoked when the button is clicked. Instead of the usual response rendering and displaying a different page, jsf.ajax.request is used to send an asynchronous request to the server. This request is made on the command button's onclick event. execute and render provide a space-separated identifier of the components. execute is the list of input components whose bean setters are invoked, and render is the list of components that needs to be rendered after the asynchronous response is received.

  The ability to process only part of the view (name and password elements in this case) is referred to as partial view processing. Similarly, rendering only part of the output page (the status element in this case) is referred to as partial output rendering.

  Table 7-3 lists the possible values of the render attribute.

Table 7-3. Values for the render attribute in f:ajax

Value	Description
@all	All components on the page
@none	No components on the page; this is the default value
@this	Element that triggered the request

Value	Description
@form	All components within the enclosing form
IDs	Space-separated identifiers of the components
EL expression	EL expression that resolves to a collection of strings

The execute attribute takes a similar set of values, but the default value for the execute attribute is @this.

- The User bean has fields, setters/getters, and a simple business method:

```
@Named
@SessionScoped
public class User implements Serializable {
    private String name;
    private String password;
    private String status;

    . . .

    public void login(ActionEvent evt) {
        if (name.equals(password))
            status = "Login successful";
        else
            status = "Login failed";
    }
}
```

Note the signature of the login method. It must return void and take javax.faces.event.ActionEvent as the only parameter.

Declarative Ajax integration is enabled by using f:ajax. This tag may be nested within a single component (enabling Ajax for a single component), or it may be "wrapped" around multiple components (enabling Ajax for many components).

The code shown above can be updated to use this style of Ajax:

```
<h:form prependId="false">
        <h:inputText value="#{user.name}"
                     id="name"/>
        <h:inputText value="#{user.password}"
                     id="password"/>
```

```
        <h:commandButton value="Login"
                         type="button"
                         actionListener="#{user.login}">
            <f:ajax execute="name password"
                    render="status"/>
        </h:commandButton>

        <h:outputText value="#{user.status}"
                      id="status"/>
    </h:form>
```

In this code, `f:ajax` is used to specify the list of input elements using the **execute** attribute, and the output elements to be rendered using the **render** attribute. By default, if `f:ajax` is nested within a single component and no event is specified, the asynchronous request is fired based upon the default event for the parent component (the **onclick** event in the case of a command button).

The `f:ajax` tag may be wrapped around multiple components:

```
<f:ajax listener="#{user.checkFormat}">
    <h:inputText value="#{user.name}" id="name"/>
    <h:inputText value="#{user.password}" id="password"/>
</f:ajax>
```

In this code, `f:ajax` has a **listener** attribute and the corresponding Java method:

```
public void checkFormat(AjaxBehaviorEvent evt) {
    //. . .
}
```

This listener method is invoked for the default event for the child elements (the **valueChange** event for `h:inputText` in this case). Additional Ajax functionality may be specified on the child elements using a nested `f:ajax`.

HTTP GET

JSF provides support for mapping URL parameters in HTTP GET requests to an EL. It also provides support to generate GET-friendly URLs.

View parameters can be used to map URL parameters in GET requests to an EL. This can be done by adding the following fragment to a Facelets page:

```
<f:metadata>
    <f:viewParam name="name" value="#{user.name}"/>
</f:metadata>
```

Accessing a web application at *index.xhtml?name=jack* will:

- Get the request parameter by the name `name`.
- Convert and validate if necessary. This is achieved by a nested `f:converter` and `f:validator`, just like with any `h:inputText`. This can be done as shown:

```
<f:metadata>
    <f:viewParam name="name" value="#{user.name}">
        <f:validateLength minimum="1" maximum="5"/>
    </f:viewParam>
</f:metadata>
```

- If successful, bind it to `#{user.name}`.

The view parameters can be post-processed before the page is rendered using `f:event`:

```
<f:metadata>
    <f:viewParam name="name" value="#{user.name}">
        <f:validateLength minimum="1" maximum="5"/>
    </f:viewParam>
    <f:event type="preRenderView"
             listener="#{user.process}"/>
</f:metadata>
```

In this code, the method identified by `#{user.process}` can be used to perform any initialization required prior to rendering the page.

GET-friendly URLs are generated using `h:link` and `h:button`. The desired Facelets page is specified instead of manually constructing the URL:

```
<h:link value="Login" outcome="login"/>
```

This is translated to the following HTML tag:

```
<a href=".../faces/login.xhtml">Login</a>
```

View parameters can be easily specified:

```
<h:link value="Login" outcome="login">
    <f:param name="name" value="#{user.name}"/>
</h:link>
```

In this code, if `#{user.name}` is bound to "Jack" then this fragment is translated to the following HTML tag:

```
<a href=".../faces/login.xhtml?name=Jack">Login</a>
```

Similarly, `h:button` can be used to specify the outcome:

```
<h:button value="login"/>
```

This code will generate the following HTML tag:

```
<input
    type="button"
    onclick="window.location.href=
'/JSFSample/faces/index.xhtml'; return false;"
    value="login" />
```

Server and Client Extension Points

Converters, validators, and listeners are server-side *attached objects* that add more functionality to the components on a page. Behaviors are client-side extension points that can enhance a component's rendered content with behavior-defined scripts.

A converter converts the data entered in a component from one format to another (e.g., string to number). JSF provides several built-in converters such as `f:convertNumber` and `f:convert DateTime`. They can be applied to any editable component:

```
<h:form>
    Age: <h:inputText value="#{user.age}" id="age">
        <f:convertNumber integerOnly="true"/>
    </h:inputText>
    <h:commandButton value="Submit"/>
</h:form>
```

In this code, the text entered in the text box will be converted to an integer if possible. An error message is thrown if the text cannot be converted.

A custom converter can be easily created:

```java
@FacesConverter("myConverter")
public class MyConverter implements Converter {

    @Override
    public Object getAsObject(
                    FacesContext context,
                    UIComponent component,
                    String value) {
        //. . .
    }

    @Override
    public String getAsString(
                    FacesContext context,
                    UIComponent component,
                    Object value) {
        //. . .
    }
}
```

In this code, the methods getAsObject and getAsString perform object-to-string and string-to-object conversions between model data objects and a string representation of those objects that is suitable for rendering. The POJO implements the Converter interface and is also marked with @FacesConverter. This converter can then be used in a JSF page:

```html
<h:inputText value="#{user.age}" id="age">
    <f:converter converterId="myConverter"/>
</h:inputText>
```

The value attribute of @FacesConverter must match the value of the converterId attribute here.

A validator is used to validate data that is received from the input components. JSF provides several built-in validators such as f:validateLength and f:validateDoubleRange. These validators can be applied to any editable component:

```html
<h:inputText value="#{user.name}" id="name">
    <f:validateLength min="1" maximum="10"/>
</h:inputText>
```

In this code, the length of the entered text is validated to be between 1 and 10 characters. An error message is thrown if the length is outside the specified range.

A custom validator can be easily created:

```
@FacesValidator("nameValidator")
public class NameValidator implements Validator {

    @Override
    public void validate(
                    FacesContext context,
                    UIComponent component,
                    Object value)
        throws ValidatorException {
        //. . .
    }

}
```

In this code, the method `validate` returns if the value is successfully validated. Otherwise a `ValidatorException` is thrown. This validator can be applied to any editable component:

```
<h:inputText value="#{user.name}" id="name">
    <f:validator id="nameValidator"/>
</h:inputText>
```

The `value` attribute of `@FacesValidator` must match the value of the `id` attribute of `f:validator` here.

JSF also provides built-in integration with constraints defined using Bean Validation. Other than placing annotation constraints on the bean, no additional work is required by the developer. Any error messages because of constraint violation are automatically converted to a `FacesMessage` and displayed to the end user. `f:validateBean` may be used to specify `validationGroups` to indicate which validation groups should be taken into consideration when validating a particular component. This is explained in detail in the Bean Validation chapter.

A listener listens for events on a component. The event can be a change of value, a click of a button, a click on a link, or something else. A listener can be a method in a managed bean or a class by itself.

A `ValueChangeListener` can be registered on any editable component:

```
<h:inputText value="#{user.age}"
             id="age"
             valueChangeListener="#{user.nameUpdated}">
```

In this code, the `nameUpdated` method in the `User` bean is called when the associated form is submitted. A class-level listener can be created by implementing the `ValueChangeListener` interface and specified in the page using the `f:valueChangeListener` tag.

Unlike converters, validators, and listeners, a `behavior` enhances client-side functionality of a component by declaratively attaching scripts to it. For example, `f:ajax` is defined as a client-side behavior. This also allows you to perform client-side validation and client-side logging, show tooltips, and other similar functionality.

Custom behaviors can be defined by extending `ClientBehaviorBase` and marking with `@FacesBehavior`.

Navigation Rules

JSF defines implicit and explicit navigation rules.

Implicit navigation rules look for the outcome of an action (e.g., a click on a link or a button). If a Facelets page matching the action outcome is found, that page is then rendered:

```
<h:commandButton action="login" value="Login"/>
```

In this code, clicking on the button will render the page *login.xhtml* in the same directory.

Explicit navigation can be specified using `<navigation-rule>` in *faces-config.xml*. Conditional navigation may be specified using `<if>`:

```
<navigation-rule>
  <from-view-id>/index.xhtml</from-view-id>
  <navigation-case>
    <from-outcome>success</from-outcome>
    <to-view-id>/login.xhtml</to-view-id>
    <if>#{user.isPremium}</if>
  </navigation-case>
</navigation-rule>
```

In this code, the page navigation from *index.xhtml* to
login.xhtml only occurs if the user is a premium customer.

CHAPTER 8

SOAP-Based Web Services

SOAP-Based Web Services are defined as JSR 224, and the complete specification can be downloaded from *http://jcp.org/aboutJava/communityprocess/mrel/jsr224/index4.html*.

SOAP is an XML-based messaging protocol used as a data format for exchanging information over web services. The SOAP specification defines an envelope that represents the contents of a SOAP message and encoding rules for data types. It also defines how SOAP messages may be sent over different transport protocols, such as exchanging messages as the payload of HTTP POST. The SOAP protocol provides a way to communicate among applications running on different operating systems, with different technologies, and different programming languages.

Java API for XML-Based Web Services (JAX-WS) hides the complexity of the SOAP protocol and provides a simple API for development and deployment of web service endpoints and clients. The developer writes a web service endpoint as a Java class. The JAX-WS runtime publishes the web service and its capabilities using Web Services Description Language (WSDL). Tools provided by a JAX-WS implementation, such as `wscompile` by the JAX-WS Reference Implementation, are used to generate proxy to the service and invoke methods on it from the client code. The JAX-WS runtime converts the API calls to and from SOAP messages and sends them over HTTP, as shown in Figure 8-1.

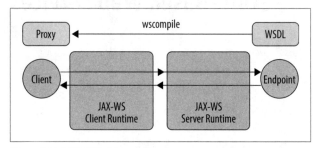

Figure 8-1. JAX-WS client and server

In addition to sending SOAP messages over HTTP, JAX-WS also provides XML-over-HTTP protocol binding and is extensible to other protocols and transports. The XML-over-HTTP binding use case is better served by JAX-RS and will not be discussed here.

Data mapping between Java and XML is defined using Java API for XML Binding (JAXB).

The JAX-WS specification defines mapping from WSDL 1.1 to Java. This mapping defines how different WSDL constructs such as `wsdl:service`, `wsdl:portType`, and `wsdl:operation` are mapped to Java. This mapping is used when generating web service interfaces for clients and endpoints from a WSDL 1.1 description.

Java to WSDL 1.1 mapping is also defined by this specification. This mapping defines how Java packages, classes, interfaces, methods, parameters, and other parts of a web service endpoint are mapped to WSDL 1.1 constructs. This mapping is used when generating web service endpoints from existing Java interfaces.

JAX-WS uses technologies defined by the W3C: HTTP, SOAP, and WSDL. It also requires compliance with the WS-I Basic Profile, the WS-I Simple SOAP Binding Profile, and the WS-I

Attachments Profile that promotes interoperability between web services. This allows a JAX-WS endpoint to be invoked by a client on another operating system written in another programming language and vice versa.

JAX-WS also facilitates, using a nonstandard programming model, the publishing and invoking of a web service that uses WS-* specifications such as WS-Security, WS-Secure Conversation, and WS-Reliable Messaging. Some of these specifications are already implemented in the JAX-WS implementation bundled as part of GlassFish. However, this particular usage of JAX-WS will not be discussed here. More details about it can be found at *http://metro.java.net*.

Web Service Endpoints

A POJO can be converted to a SOAP-based web service endpoint by adding `@WebService` annotation:

```
@WebService
public class SimpleWebService {

    public String sayHello(String name) {
        return "Hello " + name;
    }
}
```

All `public` methods of the class are exposed as web service operations.

This is called a Service Endpoint Interface (SEI)–based endpoint. Even though the name contains Interface, an interface is not required when building a JAX-WS endpoint. The web service implementation class implicitly defines an SEI. This approach of starting with a POJO is also called the *code first* approach. The other approach is where you start with a WSDL and generate Java classes from it, called the *contract first* approach.

There are reasonable defaults for `wsdl:service` name, `wsdl:portType` name, `wsdl:port` name, and other elements in the generated WSDL. The @WebService annotation has several attributes to override the defaults, as defined in Table 8-1.

Table 8-1. @WebService attributes

Attributes	Description
endpointInterface	Fully qualified class name of the service endpoint interface defining the service's abstract web service contract
name	Name of the web service (wsdl:portType)
portName	Port name of the web service (wsdl:port)
serviceName	Namespace for the web service (targetNamespace)
targetNamespace	Service name of the web service (wsdl:service)
wsdlLocation	Location of a predefined WSDL describing the service

The @WebMethod annotation can be used on each method to override the corresponding default values:

```
@WebMethod(operationName="hello")
public String sayHello(String name) {
    return "Hello " + name;
}
```

Specifying this annotation overrides the default name of the wsdl:operation matching this method.

Additionally, if any method is annotated with @WebMethod, all other methods of the class are implicitly not available at the SEI endpoint. Any additional methods are required to be annotated.

If there are multiple methods in the POJO and a particular method needs to be excluded from the web service description, the exclude attribute can be used:

```
@WebMethod(exclude=true)
public String sayHello(String name) {
    return "Hello " + name;
}
```

The mapping of an individual parameter of a method to WSDL can be customized using `@WebParam`, and the mapping of the return value using `@WebResult`.

The mapping of Java programming language types to and from XML definitions is delegated to JAXB. It follows the default Java-to-XML and XML-to-Java mapping for each method parameter and return type. The usual JAXB annotations can be used to customize the mapping to the generated schema:

```java
@WebService
public class ShoppingCart {
    public void purchase(List<Item> items) {
        //. . .
    }
    //. . .
}

@XmlRootElement
class Item {
    private String name;
    //. . .
}
```

In this code, `@XmlRootElement` allows the `Item` class to be converted to XML and vice versa.

By default, the generated WSDL uses the `document/literal` style of binding. This can be changed by specifying the `@SOAP Binding` annotation on the class:

```java
@WebService
@SOAPBinding(style= SOAPBinding.Style.RPC)
public class SimpleWebService {
    //. . .
}
```

The business methods can throw a service-specific exception:

```java
@WebMethod
public String sayHello(String name)
                throws InvalidNameException {
    //. . .
}
```

```
public class InvalidNameException extends Exception {
    //. . .
}
```

If this exception is thrown in the business method on the server side, it is propagated to the client side. If the exception is declared as an unchecked exception, it is mapped to `SOAPFaultException` on the client side. The `@WebFault` annotation may be used to customize the mapping of `wsdl:fault` in the generated WSDL.

By default, a message follows the *request response* design pattern where a response is received for each request. A method may follow the *fire and forget* design pattern by specifying the `@Oneway` annotation on it so that a request can be sent from the message but no response is received. Such a method must have a `void` return type and must not throw any checked exceptions:

```
@Oneway
public void doSomething() {
    //. . .
}
```

A `WebServiceContext` may be injected in an endpoint implementation class:

```
@Resource
WebServiceContext context;
```

This provides information about message context (using the `getMessageContext` method) and security information (using the `getUserPrincipal` and `isUserInRole` methods) relative to a request being served.

Provider-Based Dynamic Endpoints

A `Provider`-based endpoint provides a dynamic alternative to the SEI-based endpoint. Instead of just the mapped Java types, the complete protocol message or protocol message payload is available as `Source`, `DataSource`, or `SOAPMessage` at the endpoint. The response message also needs to be prepared using these APIs as well.

The endpoint needs to implement the `Provider<Source>`, `Provider<SOAPMessage>`, or `Provider<DataSource>` interface:

```
@WebServiceProvider
public class MyProvider implements Provider<Source> {

    @Override
    public Source invoke(Source request) {
        //. . .
    }

}
```

In this code, the SOAP body payload is available as a `Source`. `@WebServiceProvider` is used to associate the class with a `wsdl:service` and a `wsdl:port` element in the WSDL document.

Table 8-2 describes the attributes that can be used to provide additional information about the mapping.

Table 8-2. @WebServiceProvider attributes

Attribute	Description
portName	Port name
serviceName	Service name
targetNamespace	Target namespace for the service
wsdlLocation	Location of the WSDL for the service

By default, only the message payload (i.e., the SOAP body in the case of the SOAP protocol) is received at the endpoint and sent in a response. The `ServiceMode` annotation can be used to override this if the provider endpoint wishes to send and receive the entire protocol message:

```
@ServiceMode(ServiceMode.Mode.MESSAGE)
public class MyProvider implements Provider<Source> {
    //. . .
}
```

In this code, the complete SOAP message is received and sent from the endpoint.

`Provider<Source>` is the most commonly used `Provider`-based endpoint. A `Provider<SOAP message>` in PAYLOAD mode is not valid because the entire SOAP message is received, not just the payload that corresponds to the body of the SOAP message.

The runtime catches the exception thrown by a `Provider` endpoint and converts it to a protocol-specific exception (e.g., `SOAPFaultException` for the SOAP protocol).

Endpoint-Based Endpoints

An `Endpoint`-based endpoint offers a lightweight alternative to create and publish an endpoint. This is a convenient way of deploying a JAX-WS-based web service endpoint from Java SE applications.

A code-first endpoint can be published:

```
@WebService
public class SimpleWebService {

    public String sayHello(String name) {
        return "Hello " + name;
    }
}

//. . .

Endpoint endpoint =
    Endpoint.publish("http://localhost:8080" +
                            "/example/SimpleWebService",
                        new SimpleWebService());
```

In this code, a POJO annotated with `@WebService` is used as the endpoint implementation. The address of the endpoint is passed as an argument to `Endpoint.publish`. This method call publishes the endpoint and starts accepting incoming requests.

The endpoint can be taken down and stop receiving incoming requests:

```
endpoint.stop();
```

The endpoint implementation can be a `Provider`-based endpoint as well.

A mapped WSDL is automatically generated by the underlying runtime in this case.

A contract-first endpoint can be published by packaging the WSDL and specifying the `wsdl:port` and `wsdl:service` as part of the configuration:

```
Endpoint endpoint = Endpoint.create
(new SimpleWebService());

List<Source> metadata = new ArrayList<Source>();
Source source = new StreamSource(new InputStream(...));
metadata.add(source);
endpoint.setMetadata(metadata);

Map<String, Object> props = new HashMap<String, Object>();
props.put(Endpoint.WSDL_PORT, new QName(...));
props.put(Endpoint.WSDL_SERVICE, new QName(...));
endpoint.setProperties(props);

endpoint.publish("http://localhost:8080" +
                 "/example.com/SimpleWebService");
```

An `Executor` may be set on the endpoint to gain better control over the threads used to dispatch incoming requests:

```
ThreadPoolExecutor executor = new
ThreadPoolExecutor(4, 10, 100,
    TimeUnit.MILLISECONDS, new PriorityBlockingQueue());
endpoint.setExecutor(executor);
```

`EndpointContext` allows multiple endpoints in an application to share any information.

Web Service Client

The contract between the web service endpoint and a client is defined using WSDL. Like an SEI-based web service endpoint, a high-level web service client can be easily generated by importing the WSDL. Such tools follow the WSDL-to-Java mapping defined by the JAX-WS specification and generate the corresponding classes.

Table 8-3 describes the mapped Java artifact names generated for some of the WSDL elements.

Table 8-3. WSDL-to-Java mappings

WSDL element	Java class
wsdl:service	Service class extending javax.xml.ws.Service; provides the client view of a web service.
wsdl:portType	Service endpoint interface.
wsdl:operation	Java method in the corresponding SEI.
wsdl:input	Wrapper or nonwrapper style Java method parameters.
wsdl:output	Wrapper or nonwrapper style Java method return value.
wsdl:fault	Service-specific exception.
XML schema elements in wsdl:types	As defined by XML-to-Java mapping in the JAXB specification.

A new instance of the proxy can be generated by calling one of the getPort methods on the generated Service class:

```
@WebServiceClient(name="...",
                  targetNamespace="...",
                  wsdlLocation="...")
public class SimpleWebServiceService
    extends Service {

    URL wsdlLocation = ...
    QName serviceQName = ...

    public SimpleWebService() {
        super(wsdlLocation, serviceQName);
    }

    //. . .

    public SimpleWebService getSimpleWebServicePort() {
        return super.getPort(portQName,
                             SimpleWebService.class);
    }
}
```

A client will then invoke a business method on the web service:

```
SimpleWebServiceService service =
    new SimpleWebServiceService();
SimpleWebServicePort port =
    service.getSimpleWebServicePort();
port.sayHello("Duke");
```

A more generic `getPort` method may be used to obtain the endpoint:

```
SimpleWebServiceService service =
    new SimpleWebServiceService();
SimpleWebServicePort port = service.getPort(
                            SimpleWebService.class);
port.sayHello("Duke");
```

Each generated proxy implements the `BindingProvider` interface. Table 8-4 describes the properties that may be set on the provider.

Table 8-4. BindingProvider properties

Property name	Description
ENDPOINT_ADDRESS_PROPERTY	Target service endpoint address.
USERNAME_PROPERTY	Username for HTTP basic authentication.
PASSWORD_PROPERTY	Password for HTTP basic authentication.
SESSION_MAINTAIN_PROPERTY	Boolean property to indicate whether the client is participating in a session with service endpoint.
SOAPACTION_USE_PROPERTY	Controls whether SOAPAction HTTP header is used in SOAP/HTTP requests; default value is false.
SOAPACTION_URI_PROPERTY	Value of SOAPAction HTTP header; default value is empty string.

Typically, a generated client has an endpoint address preconfigured based upon the value of the `soap:address` element in the WSDL. The `ENDPOINT_ADDRESS_PROPERTY` can be used to target the client to a different endpoint:

```
BindingProvider provider = (BindingProvider)port;
port.getRequestContext().put(
```

```
            BindingProvider.ENDPOINT_ADDRESS_PROPERTY,
            "http://example.com/NewWebServiceEndpoint");
```

Dispatch-Based Dynamic Client

A Dispatch-based endpoint provides a dynamic alternative to
the generated proxy-based client. Instead of just the mapped
Java types, the complete protocol message or protocol message
payload is prepared using XML APIs.

The client can be implemented using Dispatch<Source>, Dis
patch<SOAPMessage>, Dispatch<DataSource>, or Dispatch<JAXB
Object>:

```
QName serviceQName = new QName("http://example.com",
                               "SimpleWebServiceService");
Service service = Service.create(serviceQName);

QName portQName = new QName("http://example.com",
                            "SimpleWebService");
Dispatch<Source> dispatch = service.createDispatch(
                                    portQName,
                                    Source.class,
                                    Service.Mode.PAYLOAD);
//. . .
Source source = new StreamSource(...);
Source response = dispatch.invoke(source);
```

In this code, a Service is created by specifying the fully qualified
QName, a port is created from the service, a Dispatch<Source> is
created, and the web service endpoint is invoked. The business
method invoked on the service endpoint is dispatched based
upon the received SOAP message.

A pregenerated Service object, generated by a tool following
WSDL-to-Java mapping, may be used to create the Dispatch
client as well.

A Dispatch<SOAPMessage> can be created:

```
Dispatch<SOAPMessage> dispatch =
    service.createDispatch(portQName,
                           SOAPMessage.class,
                           Service.Mode.MESSAGE);
```

The value of `Service.Mode` must be `MESSAGE` for `Dispatch<SOAP Message>`.

JAXB objects generated from XML-to-Java mapping may be used to create and manipulate XML representations. Such a `Dispatch` client can be created:

```
Dispatch<Object> dispatch =
    service.create(portQName,
                   jaxbContext,
                   Service.Mode.MESSAGE);
```

In this code, `jaxbContext` is the `JAXBContext` used to marshall and unmarshall messages or message payloads.

A `Dispatch` client can also be invoked asynchronously:

```
Response<Source> response = dispatch.invoke(...);
```

The `Response` object can then be used to query (using the `isDone` method), cancel (using the `cancel` method), or obtain the results from (using `get` methods) the method invocation. The asynchronous invocation may be converted into a blocking request by invoking `response.get` right after obtaining the response object.

An asynchronous request may be made using a callback:

```
Future<?> response =
    dispatch.invokeAsync(source, new MyAsyncHandler());

//. . .

class MyAsyncHandler implements AysnchHandler<Source> {
    @Override
    public void handleResponse(Response<Source> res) {
        //. . .
    }
}
```

A new class, `MyAsyncHandler`, registers a callback class that receives when the response is received from the endpoint. The `response` can be used to check if the web service invocation has completed, wait for its completion, or retrieve the result. The `handleResponse` method of the callback is used to process the response received.

A one-way request using a `Dispatch`-based client may be made:

```
dispatch.invokeOneWay(source);
```

Handlers

Handlers are well-defined extension points that perform additional processing of the request and response messages. They can be easily plugged into the JAX-WS runtime. There are two types of handlers:

Logical handler
> Logical handlers are protocol-agnostic and cannot change any protocol-specific parts of a message (such as headers). Logical handlers act only on the payload of the message.

Protocol handler
> Protocol handlers are specific to a protocol and may access or change the protocol-specific aspects of a message.

Logical handlers can be written by implementing `Logical Handler`:

```java
public class MyLogicalHandler implements LogicalHandler {
    @Override
    public boolean handleMessage(MessageContext context) {
        Source source =
            ((LogicalMessageContext)context)
            .getMessage()
            .getPayload();
        //. . .
        return true;
    }

    @Override
    public boolean handleFault(MessageContext context) {
        //. . .
    }

    @Override
    public void close(MessageContext context) {
        //. . .
    }
}
```

In this code, the handler has implemented the `handleMessage`, `handleFault`, and `close` methods. The `handleMessage` method is called for inbound and outbound message processing and the `handleFault` method is invoked for fault processing. The `handleMessage` and the `handleFault` messages return `true` to continue further processing and `false` to block processing.

`MessageContext` provides a context about the message that is currently being processed by the handler instance. It provides a predefined set of properties that can be used to communicate among different handlers. Properties are scoped to `APPLICATION` or `HANDLER`.

The message payload may be obtained as a JAXB object:

```
LogicalMessage message = context.getMessage();
Object jaxbObject = message.getPayload(jaxbContext);
// Update the JAXB Object
message.setPayload(modifiedJaxbObject,jaxbContext);
```

In this code, `jaxbObject` is obtained as the payload, updated, and then sent back explicitly as the payload on the message.

Protocol handlers, specific to the SOAP protocol, are called by the SOAP handler:

```
public class MySOAPHandler implements SOAPHandler {

    @Override
    public Set getHeaders() {
        //. . .
    }

    @Override
    public boolean handleMessage(MessageContext context) {
        SOAPMessage message =
((SOAPMessageContext) context).getMessage();
        //. . .
        return true;
    }

    @Override
    public boolean handleFault(MessageContext context) {
        //. . .
    }
```

```
    @Override
    public void close(MessageContext context) { }
}
```

In this code, the handler has implemented the `handleMessage`, `handleFault`, `close`, and `getHeaders` methods. SOAP handlers are generally used to process SOAP-specific information, such as SOAP headers. The `getHeaders` method returns the set of SOAP headers processed by this handler instance.

Handlers can be organized in a *handler chain*. The handlers within a handler chain are invoked each time a message is sent or received. Inbound messages are processed by handlers prior to dispatching a request to the service endpoint or returning a response to the client. Outbound messages are processed by handlers after a request is sent from the client or a response is returned from the service endpoint.

During runtime, the handler chain is reordered such that logical handlers are executed before the SOAP handlers on an outbound message and SOAP handlers are executed before logical handlers on an inbound message.

The sequence of logical and SOAP handlers during a request and response is shown in Figure 8-2.

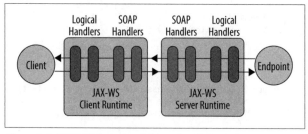

Figure 8-2. JAX-WS logical and SOAP handlers

CHAPTER 9

RESTful Web Services

RESTful web services are defined as JSR 311, and the complete specification can be downloaded from *http://jcp.org/aboutJava/communityprocess/mrel/jsr311/index.html*.

REST is an architectural style of services that utilizes web standards. Web services designed using REST are called RESTful web services. The main principles of RESTful web services are:

- Everything can be identified as a resource and each resource is uniquely identifiable using a URI.

- A resource can be represented in multiple formats, defined by a media type. The media type will provide enough information on how the requested format needs to be generated. Standard methods are defined for the client and server to negotiate on the content type of the resource.

- Use standard HTTP methods to interact with the resource: GET to retrieve a resource, POST to create a resource, PUT to update a resource, and DELETE to remove a resource.

- Communication between the client and the endpoint is stateless. All the associated state required by the server is passed by the client in each invocation.

Java API for RESTful web services (JAX-RS) defines a standard annotation-driven API that helps developers build a RESTful web service in Java. The standard principles of REST, such as identifying a resource as a URI, a well-defined set of methods to access the resource, and multiple representation formats of a resource, can be easily marked in a POJO using annotations.

Simple RESTful Web Services

A simple RESTful web service can be defined using `@Path`:

```
@Path("orders")
public class Orders {
  @GET
  public List<Order> getAll() {
    //. . .
  }

  @GET
  @Path("{oid}")
  public Order getOrder(@PathParam("oid")int id) {
    //. . .
  }
}

@XmlRootElement
public class Order {
  int id;
  //. . .
}
```

In this code:

- `Orders` is a POJO class and is published as a RESTful resource at `orders` path by adding the class-level `@Path` annotation.

- The `Order` class is marked with the `@XmlRootElement` annotation, allowing a conversion between Java and XML.

- The `getAll` resource method, providing a list of all orders, is invoked when this resource is accessed using the HTTP GET method; this is identified by specifying the `@GET` annotation on the method.

- The `@Path` annotation on the `getOrder` resource method marks it as a subresource and accessible at `orders/{oid}`.

- The curly braces around **oid** identifies it as a template parameter, and binds its value at runtime to the **id** parameter of the **getOrder** resource method.
- The **@PathParam** can also be used to bind template parameters to a resource class field as well.

Typically, a RESTful resource is bundled in a *.war* file along with other classes and resources. The **Application** class and **@ApplicationPath** annotation is used to specify the base path for all the RESTful resources in the packaged archive. The **Application** class also provides additional metadata about the application.

Let's say this POJO is packaged in the *store.war* file, deployed at **localhost:8080**, and the **Application** class is defined:

```
@ApplicationPath("webresources")
public class ApplicationConfig extends Application {
}
```

A list of all the orders is accessible by issuing a GET request to:

http://localhost:8080/store/webresources/orders

A specific order can be obtained by issuing a GET request to:

http://localhost:8080/store/webresources/orders/1

Here, the value **1** will be passed to **getOrder**'s method parameter **id**. The resource method will locate the order with the correct order number and return back the **Order** class. Having **@XmlRootElement** annotation ensures that an XML representation of the resource is returned back.

A URI may pass HTTP query parameters using name/value pairs. These can be mapped to resource method parameters or fields using **@QueryParam** annotation. If the resource method **getAll** is updated such that the returned results start from a specific order number, the number of orders returned can also be specified:

```
public List<Order> getAll(@QueryParam("start")int from,
                          @QueryParam("page")int page) {
    //. . .
}
```

And the resource is accessed as:

```
http://localhost:8080/store/webresources/orders?
    start=10&page=20
```

Then 10 is mapped to the `from` parameter and 20 is mapped to the `page` parameter.

Binding HTTP Methods

JAX-RS provides support for binding standard HTTP GET, POST, PUT, DELETE, HEAD, and OPTIONS methods using the corresponding annotations described in Table 9-1.

Table 9-1. HTTP methods supported by JAX-RS

HTTP method	JAX-RS annotation
GET	@GET
POST	@POST
PUT	@PUT
DELETE	@DELETE
HEAD	@HEAD
OPTIONS	@OPTIONS

Let's take a look at how @POST is used. Consider the following HTML form, which takes the order identifier and customer name and creates an order by posting the form to `webresources/orders/create`:

```
<form method="post" action="webresources/orders/create">
  Order Number: <input type="text" name="id"/><br/>
  Customer Name: <input type="text" name="name"/><br/>
  <input type="submit" value="Create Order"/>
</form>
```

The updated resource definition uses the following annotations:

```
@POST
@Path("create")
@Consumes("application/x-www-form-urlencoded")
```

```
public Order createOrder(@FormParam("id")int id,
                         @FormParam("name")String name) {
  Order order = new Order();
  order.setId(id);
  order.setName(name);
  return order;
}
```

The @FormParam annotation binds the value of an HTML form parameter to a resource method parameter or a field. The name attribute in the HTML form and the value of the @FormParam annotation are exactly the same to ensure the binding. Clicking the submit button in this form will return the XML representation of the created Order. A Response object may be used to create a custom response.

The following code shows how @PUT is used:

```
@PUT
@Path("{id}")
@Consumes("*/xml")
public Order putXml(@PathParam("id")int id,
                    String content) {
  Order order = findOrder(id);
  // update order from "content"
  . . .
  return order;
}
```

The resource method is marked as a subresource and {id} is bound to the resource method parameter id. The contents of the body can be any XML media type as defined by @Consumes and are bound to the content method parameter. A PUT request to this resource may be issued as:

```
curl -i -X PUT -d "New Order"
    http://localhost:8080/store/webresources/orders/1
```

The content method parameter will have the value New Order.

Similarly, an @DELETE resource method can be defined:

```
@DELETE
@Path("{id}")
public void putXml(@PathParam("id")int id) {
  Order order = findOrder(id);
```

```
    // delete order
  }
```

The resource method is marked as a subresource and {id} is bound to the resource method parameter id. A DELETE request to this resource may be issued as:

```
curl -i -X DELETE
    http://localhost:8080/store/webresources/orders/1
```

The content method parameter will have the value New Order.

The HEAD and OPTIONS methods receive automated support from JAX-RS.

The HTTP HEAD method is identical to GET except that no response body is returned. This method is typically used to obtain meta-information about the resource without requesting the body. The set of HTTP headers in response to a HEAD request is identical to the information sent in response to a GET request. If no method is marked with @HEAD, an equivalent @GET method is called and the response body is discarded. The @HEAD annotation is used to mark a method serving HEAD requests:

```
@HEAD
@Path("{id}")
public void headOrder(@PathParam("id")int id) {
  System.out.println("HEAD");
}
```

This method is often used for testing hypertext links for validity, accessibility, and recent modification. A HEAD request to this resource may be issued as:

```
curl -i -X HEAD
    http://localhost:8080/store/webresources/orders/1
```

The HTTP response header contains HTTP/1.1 204 No Content and no content body.

The HTTP OPTIONS method requests for communication options available on the request/response identified by the URI. If no method is designated with @OPTIONS, the JAX-RS runtime generates an automatic response using the annotations on the matching resource class and methods. The default response typically works in most cases. `@OPTIONS` may be used to customize the response to the OPTIONS request:

```
@OPTIONS
@Path("{id}")
  public Response options() {
  // create a custom Response and return
}
```

An OPTIONS request to this resource may be issued as:

```
curl -i -X OPTIONS
    http://localhost:8080/store/webresources/orders/1
```

The HTTP `Allow` response header provides information about the HTTP operations permitted. The `Content-Type` header is used to specify the media type of the body, if any is included.

In addition to the standard set of methods supported with corresponding annotations, `HttpMethod` may be used to build extensions such as WebDAV.

Multiple Resource Representations

By default, a RESTful resource is published or consumed with */* MIME type. A RESTful resource can restrict the media types supported by request and response using the `@Consumes` and `@Produces` annotations, respectively. These annotations may be specified on the resource class or a resource method. The annotation specified on the method overrides any on the resource class.

Here is an example showing how `Order` can be published using multiple MIME types:

```
@GET
@Path("{oid}")
@Produces({"application/xml", "application/json"})
public Order getOrder(@PathParam("oid")int id) { . . . }
```

The resource method can generate an XML or JSON representation of `Order`. The exact return type of the response is determined by the HTTP `Accept` header in the request.

Wildcard pattern matching is supported as well. The following resource method will be dispatched if the HTTP `Accept` header specifies any `application` MIME type such as `application/xml`, `application/json`, or any other media type:

```
@GET
@Path("{oid}")
@Produces("application/*")
public Order getOrder(@PathParam("oid")int id) { . . . }
```

Here is an example of how multiple MIME types may be consumed by a resource method:

```
@POST
@Path("{oid}")
@Consumes({"application/xml", "application/json"})
public Order getOrder(@PathParam("oid")int id) { . . . }
```

The resource method invoked is determined by the HTTP `Content-Type` header of the request.

A mapping between a custom representation and a corresponding Java type can be defined by implementing the `MessageBodyReader` and `MessageBodyWriter` interfaces and annotating with `@Provider`.

Binding Request to a Resource

By default, a new resource is created for each request to access the resource. The resource method parameters, fields, or bean properties are bound using *xxx*Param annotations during object creation time. In addition to `@PathParam` and `@QueryParam`, the following annotations can be used to bind different parts of the request to a resource method parameter, field, or bean property:

- `@CookieParam` binds the value of a cookie:

```
public Order getOrder(
   @CookieParam("JSESSIONID")String sessionid) {
  //. . .
}
```

This code binds the value of the `"JSESSIONID"` cookie to the resource method parameter `sessionid`.

- `@HeaderParam` binds the value of an HTTP header:

```java
public Order getOrder(
    @HeaderParam("Accept")String accept) {
  //. . .
}
```

- `@FormParam` binds the value of a form parameter contained within a request entity body. Its usage is displayed in an earlier section.

- `@MatrixParam` binds the name/value parameters in the URI path:

```java
public List<Order> getAll(
    @MatrixParam("start")int from,
    @MatrixParam("page")int page) {
  //. . .
}
```

And the resource is accessed as:

```
http://localhost:8080/store/webresources/orders;
start=10;
page=20
```

Then 10 is mapped to the `from` parameter and 20 is mapped to the `page` parameter.

More details about the application deployment context and the context of individual requests can be obtained using the `@Context` annotation.

Here is an updated resource definition where more details about the request context are displayed before the method is invoked:

```java
@Path("orders")
public class Orders {

  @Context Application app;
  @Context UriInfo uri;
  @Context HttpHeaders headers;
  @Context Request request;
```

```java
@Context SecurityContext security;
@Context Providers providers;

@GET
@Produces("application/xml")
public List<Order> getAll(@QueryParam("start")int from,
                          @QueryParam("end")int to) {
  //. . .(app.getClasses());
  //. . .(uri.getPath());
  //. . .(headers.getRequestHeader(
      HttpHeaders.ACCEPT));
  //. . .(headers.getCookies());
  //. . .(request.getMethod());
  //. . .(security.isSecure());
  //. . .
  }
}
```

In this code:

- UriInfo provides access to application and request URI information.

- Application provides access to application configuration information.

- HttpHeaders provides access to HTTP header information either as a Map or convenience methods. Note that @HeaderParam can also be used to bind an HTTP header to a resource method parameter, field, or bean property.

- Request provides a helper to request processing and is typically used with Response to dynamically build the response.

- SecurityContext provides access to security-related information of the current request.

- Providers supplies information about runtime lookup of provider instances based on a set of search criteria.

Mapping Exceptions

An application-specific exception may be thrown from within the resource method and propagated to the client. The application can supply checked or exception mapping to an instance of the Response class. Let's say the application throws the following exception if an order is not found:

```
public class OrderNotFoundException
    extends RuntimeException {

  public OrderNotFoundException(int id) {
    super(id + " order not found");
  }

}
```

The method getOrder may look like:

```
@Path("{id}")
public Order getOrder(@PathParam("id")int id) {
  Order order = null;
  if (order == null) {
    throw new OrderNotFoundException(id);
  }
  //. . .
  return order;
}
```

The exception mapper will look like:

```
@Provider
public class OrderNotFoundExceptionMapper
    implements ExceptionMapper<OrderNotFoundException> {

  @Override
  public Response toResponse(
OrderNotFoundException exception) {
    return Response
      .status(Response.Status.PRECONDITION_FAILED)
      .entity("Response not found")
      .build();
  }

}
```

This ensures that the client receives a formatted response instead of just the exception being propagated from the resource.

CHAPTER 10

Java Message Service

Java Message Service is defined as JSR 914, and the complete specification can be downloaded from *http://jcp.org/aboutJava/ communityprocess/final/jsr914/index.html*.

Message-oriented middleware (MOM) allows sending and receiving messages between distributed systems. Java Message Service (JMS) is a MOM that provides a way for Java programs to create, send, receive, and read an enterprise messaging system's messages.

JMS defines the following concepts:

JMS Provider
> An implementation of the JMS interfaces, included in a Java EE implementation.

JMS Client
> An application or process that produces and/or receives messages. Any Java EE application component can act as a JMS client.

JMS Message
> An object that contains the data transferred between JMS clients. A JMS producer/publisher creates and sends messages. A JMS consumer/subscriber receives and consumes messages.

Administered Objects

Objects created and preconfigured by an administrator. Typically refer to JMS Destinations and Connection Factories identified by a JNDI name.

JMS supports two messaging models: *Point-to-Point* and *Publish-Subscribe*.

In the Point-to-Point model, a publisher sends a message to a specific destination, called a *queue*, targeted to a subscriber. Multiple publishers can send messages to the queue, but each message is delivered and consumed by one consumer only. Queues retain all messages sent to them until the messages are consumed or expire.

In the Publish-Subscribe model, a publisher publishes a message to a particular destination, called a *topic*, and a subscriber registers interest by subscribing to that topic. Multiple publishers can publish messages to the topic, and multiple subscribers can subscribe to the topic. By default, a subscriber will receive messages only when it is active. However, a subscriber may establish a *durable* connection, so that any messages published while the subscriber is not active are redistributed whenever it reconnects.

The publisher and subscriber are loosely coupled from each other; in fact, they have no knowledge of each other's existence. They only need to know the destination and the message format.

Different levels of quality-of-service, such as missed or duplicate messages or deliver-once, can be configured. The messages may be received synchronously or asynchronously.

A JMS message is composed of three parts:

Header

is a required part of the message and is used to identify and route messages. All messages have the same set of header fields. Some fields are initialized by JMS provider and others are initialized by the client on a per-message basis.

The standard header fields are defined in Table 10-1.

Table 10-1. JMS header fields

Message header field	Description
JMSDestination	Destination to which the message is sent.
JMSDeliveryMode	Delivery mode is PERSISTENT (for durable topics) or NON_PERSISTENT.
JMSMessageID	String value with the prefix "ID:" that uniquely identifies each message sent by a provider.
JMSTimestamp	Time the message was handed off to a provider to be sent. This value may be different from the time the message was actually transmitted.
JMSCorrelationID	Used to link one message to another (e.g., a response message with its request message).
JMSReplyTo	Destination supplied by a client where a reply message should be sent.
JMSRedelivered	Set by the provider if the message was delivered but not acknowledged in the past.
JMSType	Message type identifier; may refer to a message definition in the provider's respository.
JMSExpiration	Expiration time of the message.
JMSPriority	Priorty of the message.

Properties

are optional header fields added by the client. Just like standard header fields, these are name/value pairs. The value can be boolean, byte, short, int, long, float, double, and String. Producer/publisher can set these values and consumer/subscriber can use these values as selection criteria to fine-tune the selection of messages to be processed.

Properties may be either application-specific, (standard properties defined by JMS), or provider-specific. JMS-defined properties are prefixed JMSX, and provider-specific properties are prefixed with JMS_<vendor_name>.

Body

is the actual payload of the message, which contains the application data.

Different types of body messages are shown in Table 10-2.

Table 10-2. JMS message types

Message type	Description
StreamMessage	Payload is a stream of Java primitive types, written and read sequentially.
MapMessage	Payload is a set of name/value pairs; order of the entries is undefined, can be accessed randomly or sequentially.
TextMessage	Payload is a String.
ObjectMessage	Payload is a serializable Java object.
ByteMessage	Payload is a stream of uninterpreted bytes.

Sending a Message

A JMS message can be sent from a stateless session bean:

```java
@Resource(lookup = "myConnection")
ConnectionFactory connectionFactory;

@Resource(lookup = "myQueue")
Destination inboundQueue;

public void sendMessage(String text) {
    try {
        Connection connection =
            connectionFactory.createConnection();
        Session session =
            connection.createSession(false,
                                     Session.AUTO_ACKNOWLEDGE);
        MessageProducer messageProducer =
            session.createProducer(inboundQueue);
        TextMessage textMessage =
            session.createTextMessage(text);
        messageProducer.send(textMessage);
    } catch (JMSException ex) {
        //. . .
    }
}
```

In this code:

- `ConnectionFactory` is a JMS-administered object and is used to create a connection with a JMS provider. `Queue ConnectionFactory` or `TopicConnectionFactory` may be injected instead to perform `Queue`- or `Topic`-specific operations, respectively. `Destination` is also an administered object and encapsulates a provider-specific address. A `Queue` or `Topic` may be injected here instead. Both of these objects are injected using `@Resource` and specifying the JNDI name of the resource.

- A `Connection` is created that represents an active connection to the provider. The `connection` must be closed explicitly.

- A `Session` object is created from the `connection` that provides a transaction in which the producers and consumers send and receive messages as an atomic unit of work. The first argument to the method indicates whether the session is transacted; the second argument indicates whether the consumer or the client will acknowledge any messages it receives, and is ignored if the session is transacted.

  If the session is transacted, as indicated by a `true` value in the first parameter, then an explicit call to `Session.commit` is required in order for the produced messages to be sent and for the consumed messages to be acknowledged. A transaction rollback, initiated by `Session.rollback`, means that all produced messages are destroyed, and consumed messages are recovered and redelivered unless they have expired.

  The second argument indicates the acknowledgment mode of the received message. The permitted values are defined in Table 10-3.

Table 10-3. JMS message acknowledgment mode

Acknowledgment mode	Description
`Session.AUTO_ACKNOWLEDGE`	Session automatically acknowledges a client's receipt of a message either when the session has successfully returned from a call to `receive` or when the `Message Listener` session has called to process the message returns successfully.
`Session.CLIENT_ACKNOWLEDGE`	Client explicitly calls the `Message.acknowledge` method to acknowledge all consumed messages for a session.
`Session.DUPS_OK_ACKNOWLEDGE`	Instructs the session to lazily acknowledge the delivery of messages. This will likely result in the delivery of some duplicate messages (with the `JMSRedelivered` message header set to `true`). However, it can reduce the session overhead by minimizing the work the session does to prevent duplicates.

The `session` must be explicitly closed.

- Use the `session` and the injected `Destination` object, `inboundQueue` in this case, to create a `MessageProducer` to send messages to the specified destination. A `Topic` or `Queue` may be used as the parameter to this method, as both inherit from `Destination`.

- Use one of the `Session.createXXXMessage` methods to create an appropriate message.

- Send the message using `messageProducer.send(...)`.

This code can be used to send messages using both messaging models.

Quality of Service

By default, a JMS provider ensures that a message is not lost in transit in case of a provider failure. This is called a *durable* publisher/producer. The messages are logged to stable storage for recovery from a provider failure. However, this has performance overheads and requires additional storage for persisting the messages. If a receiver can afford to miss the messages, NON_PERSISTENT delivery mode may be specified. This does not require the JMS provider to store the message or otherwise guarantee that it is not lost if the provider fails.

This delivery mode can be specified:

```
messageProducer.setDeliveryMode(
    DeliveryMode.NON_PERSISTENT);
```

All messages sent by this messageProducer follow the semantics defined by NON_PERSISTENT delivery mode.

Delivery mode may alternatively be specified for each message:

```
messageProducer.send(textMessage,
    DeliveryMode.NON_PERSISTENT, 6, 5000);
```

In this code, textMessage is the message to be sent with the NON_PERSISTENT delivery mode. The third argument defines the priority of the message and the last argument defines the expiration time.

JMS defines priority of a message on a scale of 0 (lowest) to 9 (highest). By default, the priority of a message is 4 (Message.DEFAULT_PRIORITY). Message priority may also be changed by invoking the Message.setJMSPriority method.

By default, a message never expires, as defined by Message.DEFAULT_TIME_TO_LIVE. This can be changed by calling the Message.setJMSExpiration method.

Receiving a Message Synchronously

A JMS message can be received synchronously:

```java
@Resource(lookup = "myConnection")
ConnectionFactory connectionFactory;

@Resource(lookup = "myQueue")
Destination inboundQueue;

public void receiveMessage() {
    try {
        Connection connection =
            connectionFactory.createConnection();
        Session session =
            connection.createSession(false,
                                Session.AUTO_ACKNOWLEDGE);
        MessageConsumer consumer =
            session.createConsumer(inboundQueue);
        connection.start();
        while (true) {
            Message m = consumer.receive();
            // process the message
        }
    } catch (JMSException ex) {
        //. . .
    }
}
```

In this code:

- ConnectionFactory and Destination are administered objects and are injected by the container by using the specified JNDI name. This is similar to what is done during message sending.

- As done during message sending, a Connection object and a Session object are created. Instead of creating Message Producer, a MessageConsumer is created from session and is used for receiving a message.

- In an infinite loop, consumer.receive waits for a synchronous receipt of the message.

There are multiple publishers and subscribers to a topic. The subscribers receive the message only when they are active. However, a durable subscriber may be created that receives messages published while the subscriber is not active:

```
@Resource(lookup = "myTopicConnection")
TopicConnectionFactory topicConnectionFactory;

@Resource(lookup = "myTopic")
Topic myTopic;

public void receiveMessage() {
    TopicConnection connection =
        topicConnectionFactory.createTopicConnection();
    TopicSession session =
        connection.createTopicSession(false,
                                Session.AUTO_ACKNOWLEDGE);
    TopicSubscriber subscriber =
        session.createDurableSubscriber(myTopic, "myID");
    //. . .
}
```

In this code, `TopicConnectionFactory` and `Topic` are injected using `@Resource`. `TopicConnection` is created from the factory, which is then used to create `TopicSession`. `TopicSession.createDurableSubscriber` creates a durable subscriber. This method takes two arguments: the first is the durable `Topic` to subscribe to, and the second is the name used to uniquely identify this subscription. A durable subscription can have only one active subscriber at a time. The JMS provider retains all the messages until they are received by the subscriber or expire.

A client may use `QueueBrowser` to look at messages on a queue without removing them:

```
QueueBrowser browser = session.createBrowser(inboundQueue);
Enumeration messageEnum = browser.getEnumeration();
while (messageEnum.hasMoreElements()) {
    Message message = (Message)messageEnum.nextElement();
    //. . .
}
```

Receiving a Message Asynchronously

A JMS message can be received asynchronously using a message-driven bean:

```
@MessageDriven(mappedName = "myDestination")
public class MyMessageBean implements MessageListener {

    @Override
    public void onMessage(Message message) {
        try {
            // process the message
        } catch (JMSException ex) {
            //. . .
        }
    }
}
```

In this code:

- @MessageDriven defines the bean to be a message-driven bean.

- The mappedName attribute specifies the JNDI name of the JMS destination from which the bean will consume the message. This is the same destination to which the message was targeted from the producer.

- The bean must implement the MessageListener interface, which provides only one method, onMessage. This method is called by the container whenever a message is received by the message-driven bean and contains the application-specific business logic.

This code shows how a message received by the onMessage method is a text message, and how the message body can be retrieved and displayed:

```
public void onMessage(Message message) {
    try {
        TextMessage tm = (TextMessage)message;
        System.out.println(tm.getText());
    } catch (JMSException ex) {
        //. . .
    }
}
```

Even though a message-driven bean cannot be invoked directly by a session bean, it can still invoke other session beans. A message-driven bean can also send JMS messages.

Temporary Destinations

Typically, JMS `Destination` objects (i.e., `Queue` and `Topic`) are administered objects and identified by a JNDI name. These objects can also be created dynamically, where their scope is bound to the `Connection` from which they are created:

```
TopicConnection connection =
    topicConnectionFactory.createTopicConnection();
TopicSession session =
    connection.createTopicSession(false,
                                Session.AUTO_ACKNOWLEDGE);
TemporaryTopic tempTopic =
    session.createTemporaryTopic();
```

Similarly, a `TemporaryQueue` can be created:

```
QueueConnection connection =
    queueConnectionFactory.createQueueConnection();
QueueSession session =
    connection.createQueueSession(false,
                                Session.AUTO_ACKNOWLEDGE);
TemporaryQueue tempQueue =
    session.createTemporaryQueue();
```

These temporary destinations are automatically closed, deleted, and their contents lost when the connection is closed. They can also be explicitly deleted by calling the `Temporary Queue.delete` or `TemporaryTopic.delete` method.

These temporary destinations can be used to simulate a request-reply design pattern by using `JMSReplyTo` and `JMSCor relationID` header field.

CHAPTER 11

Bean Validation

Bean Validation is defined as JSR 303, and the complete specification can be downloaded from *http://jcp.org/aboutJava/communityprocess/final/jsr303/index.html*.

Bean Validation provides a class-level constraint declaration and validation facility for Java applications.

The constraints can be declared in the form of annotations placed on a field, property, method parameter, or class. Constraints can be defined on interfaces or superclasses. Specifying a constraint on an interface ensures the constraint is enforced on classes implementing the interface. Similarly, all classes inheriting from a superclass inherit the validation behavior as well. Constraints declared on an interface or superclass are validated along with any constraints defined on the implementing or overriding class.

Validation constraints and configuration information can also be defined through XML validation descriptors in *META-INF/validation.xml*. The descriptors override and extend the metadata defined using annotations. This chapter will cover annotations-based constraint validations only.

A constraint metadata repository and an ability to query it is also available. This is primarily targeted toward tool developers as well as integration with other frameworks and libraries.

Built-in Constraints

A built-in set of constraint definitions are available that can be used on beans. Multiple constraints can be specified on a bean to ensure different validation requirements are met. These constraints can also be used for composing other constraints.

All built-in constraints are defined in the `javax.validation.constraints` package and are explained below:

`@Null`

Annotated element must be `null` and can be applied to any type:

```
@Null
String httpErrorCode;
```

The `httpErrorCode` field is capturing the HTTP status code from a RESTful endpoint.

`@NotNull`

Annotated element must not be `null` and can be applied to any type:

```
@NotNull
String name;
```

`name` is capturing the name of, say, a customer. Specifying `@NotNull` will trigger a validation error if the instance variable is assigned a `null` value.

`@AssertTrue`

Annotated element must be true and can be applied to `boolean` or `Boolean` types only:

```
@AssertTrue
boolean isConnected;
```

`isConnected` can be a field in a class managing resource connections.

`@AssertFalse`

Annotated element must be false and can be applied to `boolean` or `Boolean` types only:

```
@AssertFalse
Boolean isWorking;
```

isWorking can be a field in an Employee class.

@Min, @DecimalMin

Annotated element must be a number whose value is higher or equal to the specified minimum. `byte`, `short`, `int`, `long`, `Byte`, `Short`, `Integer`, `Long`, `BigDecimal`, and `BigInteger` are supported types:

```
@Min(10)
int quantity;
```

quantity can be a field in a class storing the quantity of stock.

@Max, @DecimalMax

Annotated element must be a number whose value is lower or equal to the specified maximum. `byte`, `short`, `int`, `long`, `Byte`, `Short`, `Integer`, `Long`, `BigDecimal`, and `BigInteger` are supported types:

```
@Max(20)
int quantity;
```

quantity can be a field in a class storing the quantity of stock.

Multiple constraints may be specified on the same field:

```
@Min(10)
@Max(20)
int quantity;
```

@Size

Annotated element size must be between the specified boundaries. `String`, `Collection`, `Map`, `Array` are supported types:

```
@Size(min=5, max9)
String zip;
```

zip can be a field capturing the zip code of a city. Length of the string is used for validation critieria. `min` and `max` define the length of the targeted field, specified values included. By default, `min` is 0 and `max` is 2147483647.

Another example is:

```
@Size(min=1)
@List<Item> items;
```

The List.size method is used for validation in this case.

@Digits

Annotated element must be a number within the accepted range. byte, short, int, long, Byte, Short, Integer, Long, BigDecimal, BigInteger, and String are supported types:

```
@Digits(integer=3,fraction=0)
int age;
```

integer defines the maximum number of integral digits and fraction defines the number of fractional digits for this number. So 1, 28, 262, and 987 are valid values. Specifying multiple constraints may make this field more meaningful:

```
@Min(18)
@Max(25)
@Digits(integer=3,fraction=0)
int age;
```

@Past

Annotated element must be a date in the past. Present time is defined as the current time according to the virtual machine. Date and Calendar are supported:

```
@Past
Date dob;
```

dob captures the date of birth.

@Future

Annotated element must be a date in the future. Present time is defined as the current time according to the virtual machine. Date and Calendar are supported:

```
@Future
Date retirementDate;
```

retirementDate stores the retirement date of an employee.

@Pattern

>Annotated string must match the specified regular expression:

```
@Pattern(regexp="[0-9]*")
String zip;
```

>zip stores the zip code of a city. The regular expression says that only digits from 0 to 9 are permitted. This field can be made more meaningful by adding the @Size constraint:

```
@Pattern(regexp="[0-9]*")
@Size(min=5, max=5)
String zip;
```

Each constraint declaration can also override the message, group, and payload fields.

message is used to override the default error message when the constraint is violated. group is used to override the default validation group, explained later. payload is used to associate metadata with the constraint.

Defining a Custom Constraint

Custom constraints designed to meet specific validation criteria can be defined by the combination of a constraint annotation and a list of custom validation implementations.

This code shows custom constraint annotation to validate a zip code:

```
@Documented
@Target({ ElementType.ANNOTATION_TYPE,
         ElementType.METHOD,
         ElementType.FIELD,
         ElementType.CONSTRUCTOR,
         ElementType.PARAMETER })
@Retention(RetentionPolicy.RUNTIME)
@Constraint(validatedBy=ZipCodeValidator.class)
@Size(min=5, message="{org.sample.zipcode.min_size}")
@Pattern(regexp="[0-9]*")
@NotNull(message="{org.sample.zipcode.cannot_be_null}")
```

```java
public @interface ZipCode {
    String message() default
        "{org.sample.zipcode.invalid_zipcode}";

    Class<?>[] groups() default {};

    Class<? extends Payload>[] payload() default {};

    Country country() default Country.US;
    public enum Country {
        US,
        CANADA,
        MEXICO,
        BRASIL
    }
}
```

In this code:

- `@Target` defines that this constraint can be declared on types, methods, fields, constructors, and method parameters.

- `@Constraint` marks the annotation to be a constraint definition. It also creates a link with its constraint validation implementation, defined by the attribute `validatedBy`. `ZipCodeValidator.class` provides the validation implementation in this case. Multiple validator implementations may be specified as an array of classes.

- `@Size`, `@Pattern`, and `@NotNull` are primitive constraints used to create this composite custom constraint. Annotating an element with `@ZipCode` (the *composed annotation*) is equivalent to annotating it with `@Size`, `@Pattern`, and `@NotNull` (the *composing annotations*) and `@ZipCode`.

  By default, each violation of a composing annotation raises an individual error report. All the error reports are collected together and each violation reported. However, `@ReportAsSingleViolation` on constraint annotation can be used to suppress the error reports generated by the composing annotations. In this case, the error report from the composed annotation is generated instead.

- `message`'s value is used to create the error message. In this case, the `message` value is a resource bundle key that enables internationalization.

- `group` specifies a validation group. This is used to perform partial validation of the bean or control the order in which constraints are evaluated. By default, the value is an empty array and belongs to the `Default` group.

- `payload` is used to associate metadata information with a constraint.

- `country` is defined as an additional element to parameterize the constraint. The possible set of values for this parameter is defined as an `enum` with the constraint definition. A default value of the parameter, `Country.US`, is also specified.

A simple zip code constraint validator implementation looks like:

```
public class ZipCodeValidator
    implements ConstraintValidator<ZipCode, String> {

    List<String> zipcodes;

    @Override
    public void initialize(ZipCode constraintAnnotation) {
        zipcodes = new ArrayList<String>();
        switch (constraintAnnotation.country()) {
            case US:
                zipcodes.add("95054");
                zipcodes.add("95051");
                zipcodes.add("94043");
                break;
            case CANADA:
                //
                break;
            case MEXICO:
                //
                break;
            case BRASIL:
                //
                break;
        }
    }
```

```
    @Override
    public boolean isValid(
        String value,
        ConstraintValidatorContext context) {
      return zipcodes.contains(value);
    }
  }
```

In this code:

- The constraint validator implementation class implements the `ConstraintValidator` interface. A given constraint can apply to multiple Java types. This requires defining multiple constraint validator implementations, one each for a specific type. This validator can only be applied to string types:

  ```
  @ZipCode
  String zip;
  ```

- The `initialize` method initializes any resources or data structures used for validation. This code initializes the array of valid zip codes for a specific country. The values of the `country` attribute and other attributes are available from the `constraintAnnotation` parameter. This method is guaranteed to be called before any use of this instance for validation.

- The `isValid` method implements the validation logic. The method returns `true` if the constraint is valid, `false` otherwise. The `value` parameter is the object to validate and `ConstraintValidatorContext` provides the context in which the constraint is executed. This method's implementation must be thread-safe. This code returns true if the zip code exists in the array of valid zip codes.

If a bean X contains a field of type Y, by default the validation of type X does not trigger the validation of type Y. However, annotating the field of type Y with `@Valid` will be cascaded along with the validation of X.

`@Valid` also provides polymorphic validation. If field Y is an interface or an abstract class, then the validation constraints applied at runtime are from the actual implementing class or subtype.

Any `Iterable` fields and properties may also be decorated with `@Valid` to ensure all elements of the iterator are validated. `@Valid` is applied recursively, so each element of the iterator is validated as well:

```
public class Order {
    @Pattern(...)
    String orderId;

    @Valid
    private List<OrderItem> items;
}
```

In this code, the list of order items is recursively validated along with the `orderId` field, because `@Valid` has been specified on `items`. If `@Valid` is not specified, only the `orderId` field is validated when the bean is validated.

Validation Groups

By default, all constraints are defined in the `Default` validation group. Also by default, all validation constraints are executed and in no particular order. A constraint may be defined in an explicitly created validation group in order to perform partial validation of the bean or control the order in which constraints are evaluated.

A validation group is defined as an interface:

```
public interface ZipCodeGroup {
}
```

This validation group can now be assigned to a constraint definition:

```
@ZipCode(groups=ZipCodeGroup.class)
String zip;
```

In this code, `zip` will be validated only when the `Zip CodeGroup` validation group is targeted for validation.

By default, the Default validation group is not included if an explicit set of groups is specified:

```
@ZipCode(groups={Default.class,ZipCodeGroup.class})
String zip;
```

Groups can inherit other groups by using interface inheritance. A new group may be defined that consists of Default and ZipCodeGroup:

```
public interface DefaultZipCodeGroup
    extends Default, ZipCodeGroup {
}
```

This new validation group can now be specified as part of the constraint, and is semantically equivalent to specifying two groups separately:

```
@ZipCode(groups=DefaultZipCodeGroup.class)
String zip;
```

Partial validation of a bean may be required when validation of certain fields is optional or resource intensive. For example, entering data in a multipage HTML form requires only the field values entered in each page to be validated. Validating previously validated fields will be redundant, and validating fields that do not yet have a value assigned will throw a validation error. This can be achieved by creating a validation group for each page:

```
public interface Page1Group {
}

public interface Page2Group {
}

public interface Page3Group {
}
```

Assign the group to the corresponding fields:

```
@Size(min=4, groups=Page1Group.class)
private String name;

@Digits(integer=3,fraction=0, groups=Page2Group.class)
int age;
```

```
@ZipCode(groups={Page3Group.class})
private String zipcode;
```

And finally, pass the validation group in the JSF page using
f:validateBean:

```
<h:form>
    Name: <h:inputText value="#{person.name}" id="name">
                <f:validateBean
    validationGroups="org.sample.Page1Group"/>
        </h:inputText>
        <h:commandButton action="index2" value="Next >"/>
</h:form>
```

The fully qualified class name of the validation group needs to
be specified in the validationGroups attribute of f:validate
Bean. Other pages will specify the corresponding validation
group.

Multiple validation groups can be specified using a comma-
separated list:

```
<h:form>
    Name:
    <h:inputText value="#{person.name}" id="name">
                <f:validateBean
    validationGroups="org.sample.Page1Group,
                      org.sample.OtherGroup"/>
        </h:inputText>
        <h:commandButton action="index2" value="Next >"/>
</h:form>
```

@GroupSequence is used to define a sequence of groups in which
the groups must be validated. This can be useful where simple
validation constraints such as @NotNull or @Size can be validated before more complex constraints are enforced:

```
@GroupSequence({Simple.class, Complex.class})
```

In this code, Simple and Complex are validation groups that are
specified on simple and complex validators of a bean. The definitions of simple and complex will depend upon the business
domain, of course.

If one of the groups from the sequence generates a constraint
violation, the subsequent groups are not processed.

Specifying @GroupSequence on a class changes the default validation group for that class.

Integration with JPA

JPA-managed classes (entities, mapped superclasses, and embeddable classes) may be configured to include validation constraints. By default, all such constraints are validated during pre-persist, pre-update, and pre-remove lifecycle events.

A JPA entity with validation constraints may be defined:

```
@Entity
public class Name {
    @NotNull
    @Size(4)
    private String name;

    @Min(16)
    @Max(25)
    private int age;

    //. . .
}
```

The default validation behavior can be changed by specifying the validation-mode element in *persistence.xml*. Its values are defined in Table 11-1.

Table 11-1. Values for validation-mode in persistence.xml

validation-mode	Description
auto	Automatic validation of entities; this is the default behavior. No validation takes place if no Bean Validation provider is found.
callback	Lifecycle validation of entities occur. An error is reported if no Bean Validation provider is found.
none	No validation is performed.

This attribute can be specified in *persistence.xml*:

```
<persistence-unit name="MySamplePU" transaction-type="JTA">
    <jta-data-source>jdbc/sample</jta-data-source>
    <exclude-unlisted-classes>
```

```
          false
      </exclude-unlisted-classes>
      <validation-mode>CALLBACK</validation-mode>
      <properties/>
  </persistence-unit>
```

These values can also be specified using the `javax.persis`
`tence.validation.mode` property if the entity manager factory
is created using `Persistence.createEntityManagerFactory`:

```
Map props = new HashMap();
props.put("javax.persistence.validation.mode", "callback");
EntityManagerFactory emf =
    Persistence.createEntityManagerFactory("MySamplePU",
                                           props);
```

By default, each entity exists in the `Default` validation group.
The `Default` group is targeted in pre-persist and pre-update
events, and no groups are targeted in pre-remove events. So the
constraints are validated when an entity is persisted or updated, but not when it is deleted.

Different validation groups may be specified for these lifecycle
events using the following properties:

- `javax.persistence.validation.group.per-persist`

- `javax.persistence.validation.group.pre-update`

These properties are used in *persistence.xml*:

- `javax.persistence.validation.group.pre-remove`

```
  <persistence-unit name="BeanValidationPU"
                             transaction-type="JTA">
      <jta-data-source>jdbc/sample</jta-data-source>
      <exclude-unlisted-classes>
        false
      </exclude-unlisted-classes>
      <validation-mode>CALLBACK</validation-mode>
      <properties>
        <property name=
            "javax.persistence.validation.group.pre-persist"
                value="org.sample.MyPrePersistGroup"/>
        <property name=
            "javax.persistence.validation.group.pre-update"
                value="org.sample.MyPreUpdateGroup"/>
```

```
        <property name=
            "javax.persistence.validation.group.pre-remove"
                value="org.sample.MyPreRemoveGroup"/>
    </properties>
</persistence-unit>
```

These properties can also be passed to `Persistence.create` `EntityManagerFactory` in a Map.

If a constraint is violated, the current transaction is marked for rollback.

Integration with JSF

A JSF application typically consists of multiple Facelets pages and corresponding backing beans to capture the data from these pages. Any constraints defined on such a backing bean are automatically validated during the *process validations* phase.

The `javax.faces.Bean` standard validator also ensures that every constraint violation that resulted in attempting to validate the model data is wrapped in a `FacesMessage` and added to the `FacesContext`. This message is then displayed to the user as other validator messages are handled.

One or more validation groups can be associated with an input tag:

```
Name:
<h:inputText value="#{person.name}" id="name">
        <f:validateBean validationGroups=
            "org.sample.Page1Group,
            org.sample.OtherGroup"/>
    </h:inputText>
    <h:commandButton action="index2" value="Next >"/>
```

This can also be used to create validation across multiple pages, as explained earlier in this chapter.

The validation groups can also be associated with a group of input tags:

```
<f:validateBean validationGroups="org.sample.MyGroup">
    <h:inputText value="#{person.name}"/>
    <h:inputText value="#{person.age}"/>
</f:validateBean>
```

In this code, the constraints are validated for the fields identified by #{person.name} and #{person.age}.

Getting Started with Java EE 6 Development and Deployment

This appendix provides a reference on how to get started with Java EE 6 programming using NetBeans IDE and GlassFish.

NetBeans IDE provides an open source, easy-to-use, and comprehensive development environment for Java EE 6 applications. GlassFish is an open source, lightweight, modular, and Java EE 6–compliant application server. Together, NetBeans and GlassFish provide a seamless out-of-the-box experience for developing, deploying, and running Java EE 6 applications.

NetBeans can be downloaded from *http://netbeans.org*. GlassFish Open Source Edition can be downloaded from *http://glass fish.org*. Note that NetBeans comes in different packaging bundles based upon the functionality available. "All" and "Java EE" bundles come prepackaged with GlassFish.

Go to *http://netbeans.org/kb/trails/java-ee.html* for an extensive list of articles, blogs, and videos to get you started with Java EE and NetBeans. The following articles will get you started with Java EE 6 development and deployment:

- Key to the Java EE 6 Platform: NetBeans IDE 7.1: *http://www.oracle.com/technetwork/articles/java/unlocking-1540042.html*
- Getting Started with Java EE 6 Applications: *http://netbeans.org/kb/docs/javaee/javaee-gettingstarted.html*
- Introduction to JavaServer Faces 2.0: *http://netbeans.org/kb/docs/web/jsf20-intro.html*
- Getting Started with Contexts and Dependency Injection and JSF 2.0: *http://netbeans.org/kb/docs/javaee/cdi-intro.html*
- Working with Injection and Qualifiers in CDI: *http://netbeans.org/kb/docs/javaee/cdi-inject.html*
- Working with Events in CDI: *http://netbeans.org/kb/docs/javaee/cdi-events.html*
- Creating an Enterprise Application with EJB 3.1: *http://netbeans.org/kb/docs/javaee/javaee-entapp-ejb.html*
- Creating an Enterprise Application Using Maven: *http://netbeans.org/kb/docs/javaee/maven-entapp.html*
- Dependency Injection with Stateless Session Beans: *http://netbeans.org/kb/samples/javaee-stateless.html*

NetBeans-related questions can be asked in NetBeans Forums at *http://forums.netbeans.org/*.

GlassFish-related questions can be asked in GlassFish Forums at *http://www.java.net/forums/glassfish/glassfish*.

Further Reading

This appendix provides a reference to the specifications for different technologies included in the Java EE 6 platform.

Web Technology Specifications

- JSR 45: Debugging Support for Other Languages: *http://jcp.org/en/jsr/detail?id=45*
- JSR 52: Standard Tag Library for JavaServer Pages (JSTL)1.2: *http://www.jcp.org/en/jsr/detail?id=52*
- JSR 245: JavaServer Pages (JSP) 2.2 and Expression Language (EL) 1.2: *http://jcp.org/en/jsr/detail?id=245*
- JSR 314: JavaServer Faces (JSF) 2.0: *http://jcp.org/en/jsr/detail?id=314*
- JSR 315: JavaServlet 3.0: *http://jcp.org/en/jsr/detail?id=315*

Enterprise Technology Specifications

- JSR 250: Common Annotations for the Java Platform 1.1: *http://jcp.org/en/jsr/detail?id=250*
- JSR 299: Contexts and Dependency Injection (CDI) for the Java EE Platform 1.0: *http://jcp.org/en/jsr/detail?id=299*

- JSR 303: Bean Validation 1.0: *http://jcp.org/en/jsr/detail?id=303*
- JSR 316: Managed Beans 1.0: *http://jcp.org/en/jsr/detail?id=316*
- JSR 317: Java Persistence API (JPA) 2.0: *http://jcp.org/en/jsr/detail?id=317*
- JSR 318: Enterprise JavaBeans (EJB) 3.1: *http://jcp.org/en/jsr/detail?id=318*
- JSR 318: Interceptors 1.1: *http://jcp.org/en/jsr/detail?id=318*
- JSR 322: Java EE Connector Architecture 1.6: *http://jcp.org/en/jsr/detail?id=322*
- JSR 330: Dependency Injection for Java 1.0: *http://www.jcp.org/en/jsr/detail?id=330*
- JSR 907: Java Transaction API (JTA) 1.1: *http://jcp.org/en/jsr/detail?id=907*
- JSR 914: Java Message Server (JMS) 1.1: *http://www.jcp.org/en/jsr/detail?id=914*
- JSR 919: JavaMail 1.4: *http://jcp.org/en/jsr/detail?id=919*

Web Service Technologies

- JSR 67: Java APIs for XML Messaging (JAXM) 1.3: *http://jcp.org/en/jsr/detail?id=67*
- JSR 93: Java API for XML Registries (JAXR) 1.0: *http://jcp.org/en/jsr/detail?id=93*
- JSR 101: Java API for XML-based RPC (JAX-RPC) 1.1: *http://jcp.org/en/jsr/detail?id=101*
- JSR 109: Implementing Enterprise Web Services 1.3: *http://jcp.org/en/jsr/detail?id=109*
- JSR 173: Streaming API for XML (StAX) 1.0: *http://www.jcp.org/en/jsr/detail?id=173*
- JSR 181: Web Services Metadata for the Java Platform 2.0: *http://jcp.org/en/jsr/detail?id=181*

- JSR 222: Java Architecture for XML Binding (JAXB) 2.2: *http://jcp.org/en/jsr/detail?id=222*
- JSR 224: Java API for XML Web Services (JAX-WS) 2.2: *http://jcp.org/en/jsr/detail?id=224*
- JSR 311: Java API for RESTful Web Services (JAX-RS) 1.1: *http://jcp.org/en/jsr/detail?id=311*

Management and Security Technologies

- JSR 77: J2EE Management API 1.1: *http://jcp.org/en/jsr/detail?id=77*
- JSR 88: Java Platform EE Application Deployment API 1.2: *http://jcp.org/en/jsr/detail?id=88*
- JSR 115: Java Authorization Contract and Containers (JACC) 1.3: *http://jcp.org/en/jsr/detail?id=115*
- JSR 196: Java Authentication Service Provider Interface for Containers (JASPIC) 1.0: *http://jcp.org/en/jsr/detail?id=196*

Index

Symbols

/ MIME type, 143

A

Accept header (HTTP), 144
AccountServlet class, 20
ActionEvent class, 112
@ActivationConfigProperty
  annotation, 65
AfterBeanDiscovery event, 97
AfterDeploymentValidation
  event, 97
Ajax technologies, 110–113
Allow header (HTTP), 143
@Alternative annotation, 83, 93
ambiguous dependency, 83
annotations (see specific
  annotations)
@Any annotation, 82
Application class, 139, 146
@ApplicationPath annotation,
  139
@ApplicationScoped annotation,
  90
@AroundInvoke annotation, 87
@AssertFalse annotation, 162

@AssertTrue annotation, 162
AsyncContext.complete method,
  30
AsyncHandler.handleResponse
  method, 133
@Asynchronous annotation, 70
asynchronous communication
  Dispatch-based dynamic
    clients and, 133
  receiving JMS messages, 158
  servlets, 29–31
  session beans, 70
AsyncListener interface, 28, 31
AsyncResult class, 71
@AttributeOverrides annotation,
  41
authentication, 35

B

Bean Validation
  about, 11, 161
  built-in constraints, 162–165
  defining custom constraints,
    165–169
  JPA and, 172–174
  JSF and, 117, 174
  validating entities, 50–52

We'd like to hear your suggestions for improving our indexes. Send email to *index@oreilly.com*.

About the Author

Arun Gupta is a Java evangelist working at Oracle. Arun has over 16 years of experience in the software industry working in the Java platform and several web-related technologies. In his current role, he works to create and foster the community around Java EE and GlassFish. He has been with the Java EE team since its inception and contributed to all releases. Arun has extensive worldwide speaking experience on myriad topics and loves to engage with the community, customers, partners, and Java User Groups everywhere to spread the goodness of Java.

He is a prolific blogger at *http://blogs.oracle.com/arungupta*, with over 13,00 blog entries and frequent visitors from around the world. He is a passionate runner and always up for running in any part of the world. You can catch him at *@arungupta*.

Colophon

The animal on the cover of *Java EE 6 Pocket Guide* is the jellyfish of the South Seas (*Favonia octonema*). Since jellyfish have been in existence for well over 500 million years, they are now the oldest multiorgan animal. They inhabit every ocean, from coastlines to the deep sea. Some types are even able to survive in fresh water. Though they are capable of living much longer, the typical lifespan of a jellyfish in the wild is a few hours to several months.

The jellyfish's distinctive body is made up of 95% water, a gelatinous body, and a group of nerves. Since they lack both a brain and a central nervous system, a jellyfish uses only its nerves to sense its surroundings. The difference in size between different types of jellyfish is substantial: the smallest species is a few millimeters in length, while some of the largest species are more than 65 meters long. The Favonia octonema has a sub-hemispherical body; at its root are eight appendages with suckers. Like all jellyfish, they are carnivorous, and typically will eat plankton, small fish, and fish eggs.

The jellyfish's natural defense mechanism is its sting. This sting comes from nematocysts—explosive cells that emit toxins. A single touch can cause millions of nematocysts to inject venom into the victim. To humans, a sting (depending on the jellyfish) might have no effect, be mildly to extremely painful, or in some cases, can be fatal.

The cover image is from Johnson's Natural History. The cover font is Adobe ITC Garamond. The text font is Linotype Birka; the heading font is Adobe Myriad Condensed; and the code font is LucasFont's TheSansMonoCondensed.